Englisch für Erwachsene

ENGLISH

FOR EUROPE

Cornelsen & OXFORD

Who is English for Europe for?

It is for adult learners who have reached approximately Stage 1 of the ICC language certificate system and who want to reach a level at which they can – if they wish – take the ICC Certificate (Stage 2) exam. But this is not just a course for people who want to prepare for an examination.

It's for you!

It is designed to help you to learn to use English for a range of social and professional purposes and to show you some of the situations in which English is used in Europe.

It is not about drinking tea, red buses or policemen with funny hats. Most English spoken in Europe does not involve English people at all. So this course is about English used by Europeans.

You may have arrived at English for Europe through a number of different routes.

1 Perhaps you were a complete beginner when you started to learn English as an adult, and perhaps you have progressed up to this level through books such as *Einstiegskurs* and *Essential English 1* and *2*.

2 Perhaps you started an adult English course as a false beginner, and you have progressed up to this level through *Essential English*.

3 Perhaps you are starting an English course directly at this level. Maybe you learned some English at school quite recently, or maybe you have some other recent experience of learning the language.

Whatever your background and whatever your aims in learning English, we hope that you will find English for Europe interesting and enjoyable. We hope that you have as much fun learning with it as we have had writing it.

Keith Morrow & John Roberts

Contents

BLOCK ONE

Prescribed Modules

1	**Interaction** Getting to know the people in your class	**Grammar** **must/mustn't/ needn't**	**Listening** Views of Europe
2	**Reading** INTEX – the structure of a multinational company	**Pronunciation** problem sounds: /w/ /θ/ /ə/ /b/ /d/ /g/ /r/	**Grammar** present simple passive
3	**Reading** Ana Vasquez: a Spaniard in Brussels	**Grammar** future continuous	**Writing** Describing what people look like
4	**Listening** A progress report at a business meeting	**Vocabulary** Countries Nationalities Job applications	**Grammar** present simple present continuous
5	**Grammar** **wouldn't/ ought to had better**	**Interaction** Arranging a meeting with someone	**Reading** The Channel Tunnel
6	**Pronunciation** /æ/ contrasted with /e/; stressed & unstressed syllables	**Grammar** past simple present perfect simple	**Writing** A letter of confirmation
7	**Reading** Three texts about a city in France	**Interaction** Stating food preferences/ dislikes Describing different dishes	**Grammar** gerunds & participles
8	**Writing** A short letter of apology Giving directions	**Listening** How to get from Gloucester to Brussels by car	**Grammar** reported speech

BLOC

Prescribed Modules

9	**Grammar** conditionals 1	**Interaction** Asking & describing: weekend plans Warning: possible problems/stating alternatives
10	**Grammar** conditionals 2	**Writing** A description from notes
11	**Listening** Telephone messages	**Grammar** indirect questions & commands
12	**Grammar** past simple & past continuous past perfect	**Reading** The Estonia disaster
13	**Grammar** quantifiers: countables & uncountables	**Interaction** Welcoming Arranging the seating Offering/ accepting/declining Saying goodbye
14	**Grammar** present perfect & past perfect: simple & continuous	**Writing** Correcting a formal letter
15	**Reading** European stereotypes	**Grammar** causative use of ***have*** & ***get***
16	**Grammar** prepositions + adjectives/ verbs nouns + verb phrases	**Listening** Weather forecast

· Overview

'WO

Module Banks

Each module can be combined with any session from 9 – 16

eading
atching newspaper
rticles with headlines

/riting
n advertisement
covering letter

teraction
esigning a flag
escribing a design

istening
addy O'Connor:
traditional Irish story

ronunciation

trong & weak forms

nking: introduction
ntrusive /j/ and /w/

'ocabulary

1eans of transport
he weather

)ccupations
'laces of work
ools

BLOCK THREE

Prescribed Modules

17	**Grammar** questions & question tags
18	**Grammar** past tense forms
19	**Grammar** ***may***, ***might***, ***could*** ***if*** & ***unless***
20	**Grammar** Uses of indefinite & definite articles
21	**Grammar** present perfect continuous ***since*** & ***for*** with negatives
22	**Grammar** modals with the perfect
23	**Grammar** review of all passive verb forms
24	**Grammar** review of language from this Block

Module Banks

Each module can be combined with any session from 17 – 24

	1	2	3
Reading	The Swiss Army Knife	Women in Europe	Attitudes to sex education
Writing	A letter from a friend	Replying to an invitation	A formal complaint
Interaction	Cross-cultural learning	Making & responding to complaints	Generalising Agreeing/ disagreeing with general-isations
Listening	Radio news	Telephoning answering machines: messages	Extended interview: working abroad
Pronunciation	variable syllable stress; rising/ falling intonation	rising/ falling intonation; spelling & telephone numbers	
Vocabulary	Containers Drinks Adjective sequence	Idioms Collocations Comparisons	

Course Book Framework

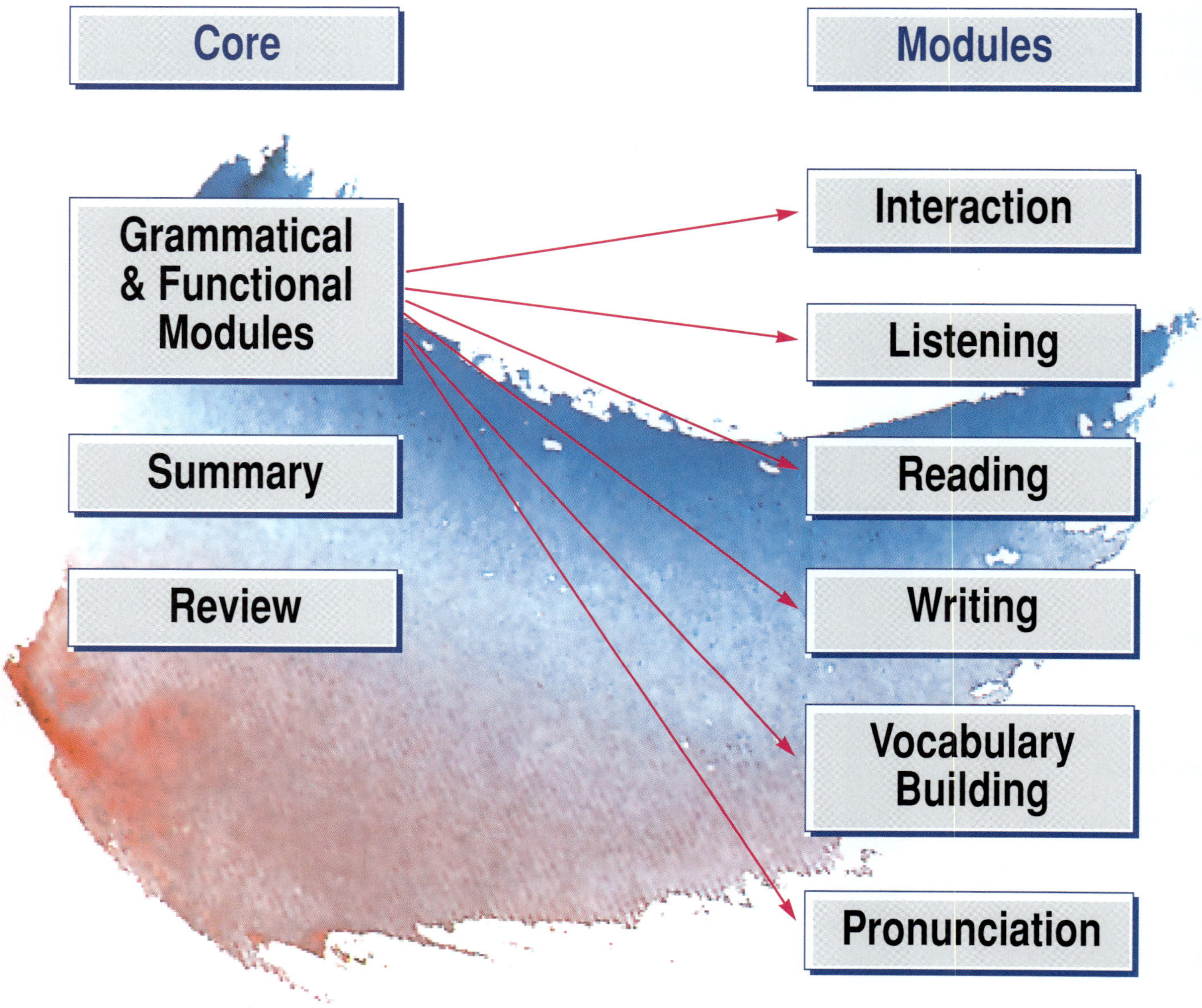

What is in English for Europe?

At the heart of the material are twenty-four grammatical/functional modules. Every lesson includes work on one of these modules, and every lesson has a Summary and a Review to help you to remember what you have learnt. At the end of each block of eight sessions there are Record and Evaluation Charts which help you to think about what you have done and the progress you have made.

As well as the grammatical core, the rest of the lesson is also made up of work on modules but in different areas. In **Block One** of the Course Book (sessions 1 – 8) the modules to be covered in each session are prescribed in the book – just like a normal text book.

But in **Block Two** (sessions 9 –16) and **Block Three** (sessions 17 – 24) you and your colleagues in the group have the chance to choose yourselves which modules you will add to the prescribed core in each session from the Module Banks. So each session can have a different shape:

Example 1:	Grammar	+	Listening	+	Writing
Example 2:	Grammar	+	Reading	+	Vocabulary
Example 3:	Grammar	+	Interaction	+	Pronunciation

You will have time to cover all sections of the Course Book in twenty-four 90-minute sessions.

Who chooses?

In **Block Two** and **Three**, you will decide with your teacher on some of the content of each session. We believe that adult learners can benefit by beginning to take responsibility for their own learning – and this can include discussion of the elements that make up an interesting and relevant session. The Course Book and the teacher will give you all the guidance you need.

You will find that the Review section of the material also asks you to make choices – about words or phrases you want to remember, and about the material you have covered. Making these choices is part of your responsibility for your learning.

Vocabulary Book

You will find with the Course Book which sets out key words and phrases for you to learn. It does not contain every word from English for Europe which you do to not know; it concentrates on the important words which you should try to learn for future use and is based on the ICC Certificate specifications.

To make the best use of English for Europe, you will also need a good dictionary. We believe that learning to use a dictionary effectively is a very important part of developing independence in learning a foreign language so you will have the opportunity to develop this skill.

Learner's Book

A Learner's Book is available to accompany English for Europe. This contains follow-up activities for every module of the Course Book.

Welcome to Block One Sessions 1 – 8

This block consists of eight 90-minute sessions of modules in a prescribed combination and sequence.

There is an overview of what you will find in this block on page 8.

Prescribed Modules

1	**Interaction** Getting to know the people in your class	**Grammar** ***must/mustn't/ needn't***	**Listening** Views of Europe
2	**Reading** INTEX – the structure of a multinational company	**Pronunciation** problem sounds: /w/ /θ/ /ð/ /b/ /d/ /g/ /r/	**Grammar** present simple passive
3	**Reading** Ana Vasquez: a Spaniard in Brussels	**Grammar** future continuous	**Writing** Describing what people look like
4	**Listening** A progress report at a business meeting	**Vocabulary** Countries Nationalities Job applications	**Grammar** present simple present continuous
5	**Grammar** ***wouldn't/ought to*** ***had better***	**Interaction** Arranging a meeting with someone	**Reading** The Channel Tunnel
6	**Pronuciation** /æ/ contrasted with /e/ stressed & unstressed syllables	**Grammar** past simple present perfect simple	**Writing** A letter of confirmation
7	**Reading** Three texts about a city in France	**Interaction** Stating food preferences/ dislikes Describing different dishes	**Grammar** gerunds & participles
8	**Writing** A short letter of apology Giving directions	**Listening** How to get from Gloucester to Brussels by car	**Grammar** reported speech

Interaction module

In this module you are going to:
- ★ practise building sentences.
- ★ practise asking and answering questions and taking notes.
- ★ use your notes to describe someone.

A Building sentences

Work on your own, then check your answers with a partner.

Here are the beginnings of twelve questions.
Try and match them with an appropriate ending from the list below.

Example
6 Which foreign country . . . c . . . would you like to live in?

1	What is the name of . . .	a	. . . like to be if you weren't a human being?
2	Which animal . . .	b	. . . person in your life?
3	What makes . . .	c	. . . would you like to live in?
4	Where were . . .	d	. . . the first foreign city you visited in Europe?
5	Which character from history . . .	e	. . . are you most afraid of?
6	Which foreign country . . .	f	. . . would you like to meet?
7	Which, in your opinion, . . .	g	. . . more than three times?
8	Which animal would you . . .	h	. . . you laugh?
9	Who is the most important . . .	i	. . . describe you best?
10	Which two adjectives . . .	j	. . . is the most beautiful European city?
11	Have you ever read a book . . .	k	. . . present you have ever had?
12	What is the best . . .	l	. . . you born?

B Asking and answering questions

Work with a partner.

Choose eight of these questions that you would like to answer about yourself. Write down the numbers on a piece of paper. Exchange your piece of paper with your partner and ask each other the questions on the list.

Take it in turns to ask the questions and make a note of your partner's answers.

C Describing your partner

Using the notes you have made about your partner, describe her/him to another member of your group. DO NOT USE YOUR PARTNER'S NAME. Can they guess who you are describing?

Grammar module must/mustn't/needn't

In this module you are going to:

- ★ look at some examples of this grammar point in action.
- ★ practise using this grammar point to talk about your own town or country.
- ★ practise using this grammar point to talk about your language learning.

A Grammar in action

People from all over Europe work at the headquarters of INTEX, in Brussels, a large multinational company. In order to help them to feel at home in Belgium, the company has produced a leaflet giving some tips.

Look at each of the tips.

Living in Brussels

You must

- open a bank account here so we can pay you.
- give three kisses when you greet a friend of the opposite sex.
- take a small gift if you are invited to someone's house.

You mustn't

- cross the road against a red light.
- drink any alcohol if you are driving. (Our police are very strict about this!)
- arrive late at a social event.

12

You needn't

- get a visa if you are a citizen of the European Union.
- use yellow bulbs in your car headlights.
- take a driving test if you are staying less than a year.

You can

- buy a weekly or monthly ticket which allows you to use all the public transport in the city.
- use your credit card from your own country here.
- get emergency medical treatment by dialling 100.

13

B Using this grammar in your situation

Work in a group of three.

1 Look at each of the tips. Is it the same in your country as in Brussels?
2 What important tips would you give to a visitor to your town about things they must do and things they mustn't do?

C Using this grammar in a new situation

Work on your own, then check your answers with a partner.

Here are some tips for people learning a foreign language. Complete each one with *you must*, *you mustn't*, or *you needn't*.

1 __________ try to practise for a short time each day. Little and often is the best way.
2 __________ try to understand every single word you read or hear. The important thing is to get the general message.
3 __________ think so much about grammar that you are frightened to speak. People will understand even if you make mistakes; if you say nothing, how can they understand?
4 __________ forget to review each lesson after you have finished. What have you learnt today?
5 __________ remember that bilingual dictionaries can be dangerous. Often a word can have more than one meaning and you may choose the wrong one in the foreign language.
6 __________ write down every new word you meet in a lesson. But do make a note of a few interesting ones. What will you do with them then?

Now add three more tips from your own experience.

Listening module

In this module you are going to:
- ★ discuss what you think about Europe.
- ★ listen to three interviews and identify specific words and phrases.

A Personal reactions

Work on your own, then with a partner.

What do you think of when you hear the word **Europe**? Make a list. Which of the things on your list do you think of as *positive* and which of the things do you think of as *negative*?

Compare your list with your partner's.

B Listening to identify specific words

Work on your own.

You are going to hear interviews with three people:
Heather, a secretary; *Sandra*, a teacher; *Idris*, a computer specialist. They all have one thing in common. They have spent part of their lives in countries outside Europe.

As you listen to the interviews, put a tick in the correct space below to show which countries each person talks about in their interview.

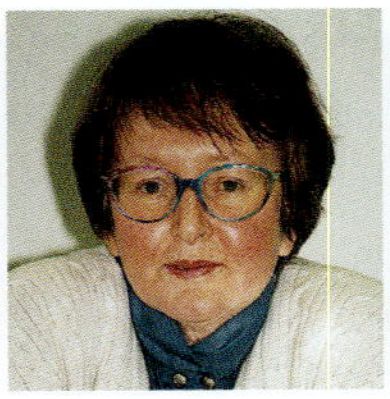

	Heather	Sandra	Idris
China			
England			
Germany			
Hong Kong			
New Zealand			
Pakistan			
Portugal			
The Bahamas			
The United States of America			
Wales			
Italy			

C Listening to identify specific phrases

Work in groups of three.

Heather, *Sandra* and *Idris* all explain what they think of when they hear the word **Europe**. Here are some of the things they said:

1 *I find it difficult to think of Europe as a single entity.*
2 *That's Europe to me, just very big and different.*
3 *. . . it's a very small part of the world which is densely-populated . . . which seems to enjoy an extremely high standard of living.*
4 *. . . many different countries, different customs, ways of life, all living very close together.*

Look at the words written in *italics*; match them with the following definitions.

Words	Definition
____________________	The level of wealth and comfort that a person, group or country has.
____________________	Ways of behaving which a group or society has had for a long time.
____________________	Something that exists separately from something else.
____________________	Containing a lot of people living close together.

Listen to the interviews again and decide who said what.
Write 1, 2, 3 or 4 next to the names. Sandra _____; Heather _____; Idris _____

D Personal Reaction

Work in groups of three.

Which of the statements is closest to your view of Europe?
Compare your views with the others in your group.

Summary

Interaction
– How many of your eight questions can you remember?
– How many of your partner's replies can you remember?

Grammar must/mustn't/needn't
– You must try to practise for a short time each day. Little and often is the best way.
– You mustn't think so much about grammar that you are frightened to speak.
– You needn't try to understand every single word you read or hear.
The important thing is to get the general message.

Listening
– What do you think of when you hear the word **Europe**?
* *I find it difficult to think of Europe as a single entity.*
▲ *That's Europe to me, just very big and different.*
● *. . . it's a very small part of the world which is densely-populated . . . which seems to enjoy an extremely high standard of living.*
▲ *. . . many different countries, different customs, ways of life, all living very close together*

– **Countries** China • Hong Kong • Pakistan • The Bahamas • Wales

Review

This review is to help you:
★ to remember what you have covered in this session.
★ to evaluate your performance and progress.
★ to identify and remember some vocabulary and language of interest to you.

Work on your own at home after the session.

1 Fill in the Record Chart and the Evaluation Chart at the end of Block One on page 51/52.
Look through the Summary for session 1 and remember the activities you did in class.

2 Write down here:
Three key words you want to remember.

__________ __________ __________

Three key phrases or structures you want to remember.

__________ __________ __________

Reading module

In this module you are going to:

- ★ locate information in one type of text and transfer it to another type of text.
- ★ find the best heading to describe what a part of a text is about.

A Locating and transferring information

Work on your own and then in a small group. Read the text about INTEX and use the information to complete the structure diagram of the company. Check your answers with your partners.

INTEX – Who are we and what do we do?

INTEX is an international company which specialises in the manufacture of nylon fibre. The company produces about a thousand different types of fibre ranging in size from fibres which are finer than a human hair to fibres which are about the same thickness as a string on a tennis racquet. INTEX has seven centres in six European countries. There are two centres that manufacture fibres in the U.K.; they are located in Gloucester and in Pontypool in South Wales. A third fibre manufacturing centre is in Lyon in South-Eastern France. The company's executive centre, INTEX International, deals with the administration of the company, sales and marketing and is located in Brussels. INTEX has a Polymer Research and Manufacturing Centre in Magdeburg in the East of Germany and it controls two subsidiary companies in The Netherlands and the North of Italy. The Dutch centre, in Rozenburg, specialises in the manufacture of carpets and other types of flooring, and the Italian centre in Como manufactures hosiery [tights and socks] and swimwear.

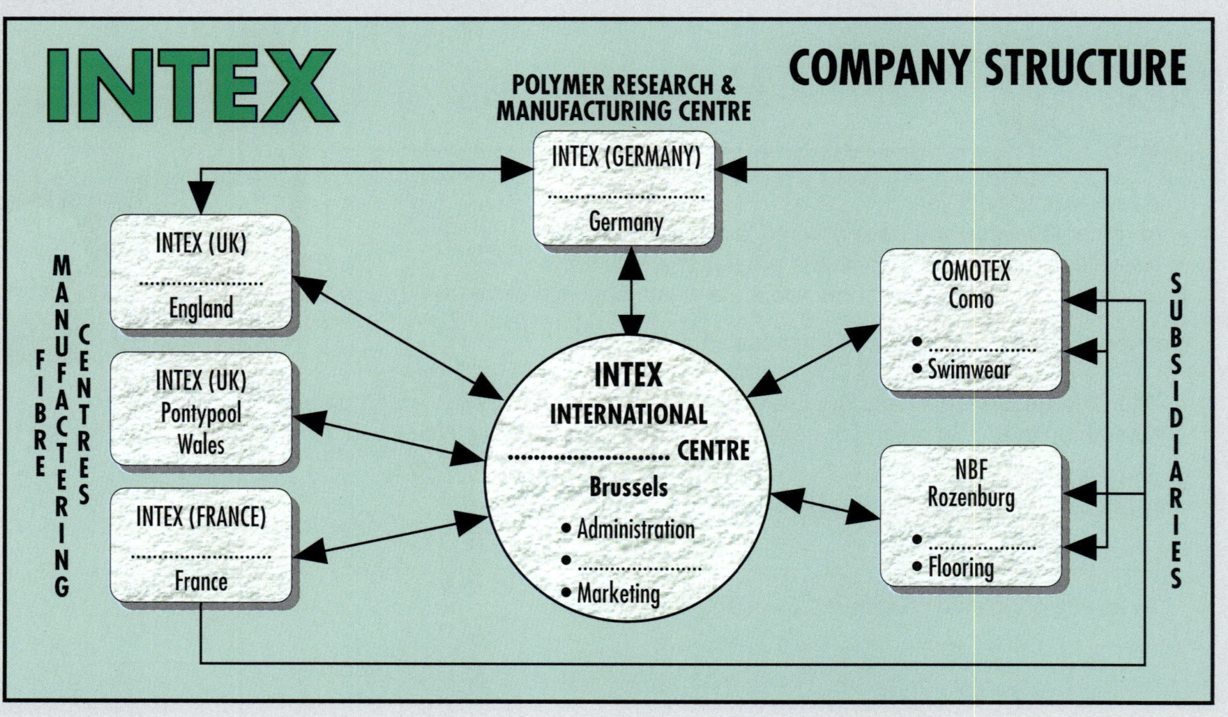

B Describing what parts of a text are about

Work in a small group.

Look at this extract from the INTEX publicity brochure. Each section needs a heading. Choose the best one from these possibilities.

Health • Transport • Flooring • Clothing • Communication

WHERE YOU FIND US

Our products are highly specialised because we have designed them that way. By producing specialised products, INTEX serves its customers. This is how we do it.

____

Whatever you wear, the chances are that we will have created a product for it. Fashion-wear, sports, leisure-wear and inner-wear. Outer garments like raincoats and anoraks. Inner garments like lingerie, socks, stockings and tights.

____

Look around your own home or office. Look around an air terminal or a conference hall. Carpets, tiles, and rugs are made from our fibres.

____

Our fibres are in hospitals and nursing homes; surgeons use sutures while wounds are protected with bandages and gauzes.

____

Our fibres help things move – safely. Tyres for cars, trucks, tractors, aircraft – even earthmovers – are reinforced with INTEX polyamide fibres.

Car interiors, too. Carpets, seats, headliners, panels – all these are made from our fibres.

____

Don't take our word for it. Ask any computer programmer or telecommunications engineer about printer ribbons, woven from strong, light INTEX polyamide yarn.

Pronunciation module

In this module you are going to:
- ★ listen to and repeat words containing these letters w, th, b, d, g, r.
- ★ practise the different ways of pronouncing the letters th and r.
- ★ compare your partner's pronunciation with the examples you hear on the cassette.
- ★ practise spelling words aloud and writing down words that are spelled aloud.

A Focus on specific sounds

Work in groups of three.

Listen to the following words read first by a native speaker of English and then by a non-native speaker of English. The pronunciation is a little different, but both people are easy to understand.

1	WILL	TOMORROW	EVERYWHERE
2	THINK	MONTH	NOTHING
3	THIS	WEATHER	WITH
4	PUB	DOUBLE	BILL
5	SAD	FRIDAY	DOWN
6	BIG	GREEN	CIGAR
7	READ	DIFFERENT	MOTHER

Each person is going to listen to the recording again and repeat the words aloud. It is difficult to hear your own errors so the other two people in the group are going to help you by writing down the words which don't sound right. When you have finished, check your errors with the other two people in your group.

Discuss which sound you find most difficult to pronounce.

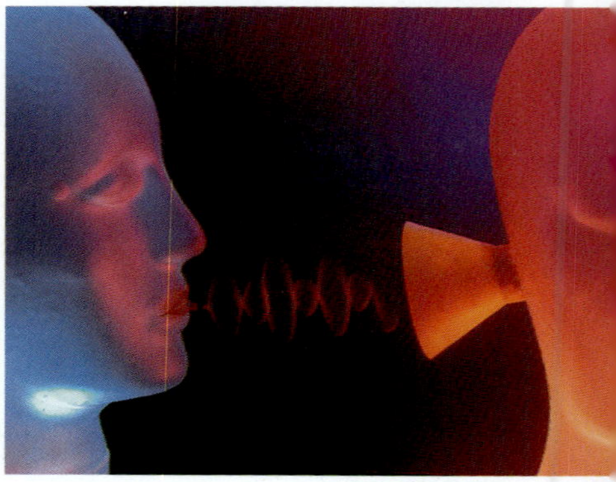

Does the sound come:
- at the beginning of the word?
- in the middle of the word?
- at the end of the word?

Try and write a sentence using as many of your problem words as possible. For example,

think • month • nothing • this • weather • with

So you think there is nothing the matter with the weather this month?

Use your sentence as a practice sentence to help you improve the pronunciation of the sounds you find difficult.

B Writing down words that are spelled aloud

Work alone.

Listen to the following short extracts from five different telephone calls and write down the information that is spelled out.

1 Family name ______________________
2 First name(s) ______________________
3 House name/number ______________
4 Street name ______________________
5 Town ____________ Post code _______

Check your answers with a partner.

C Writing down names and addresses

Work with a partner.

Ask your partner to give you the name and address of the oldest member of her/his family. Ask her/him to spell the names for you.

Grammar module the passive

In this module you are going to:
- look at some examples of this grammar point in action.
- practise using this grammar to describe how some food is prepared.
- answer and ask some quiz questions about food and drink.

A Grammar in action

Work in a small group.

Everybody can cook pasta. But this recipe has been mixed up. Number the stages to make pasta.

Pasta

Ingredients required: 3 litres water; 300g pasta; salt; oil

___ The salt is added to the water.
___ The heat is turned down and the pasta is cooked gently until it has been softened.
___ The salted water is brought to the boil.
___ The oil is added to the water. (Butter can be used instead of oil if preferred.)
___ The pasta is added to the boiling water.

The pasta can be served with a sauce or just with a dressing of oil.

B Using this grammar in your situation

Work in a small group.

How is your favourite dish made? What are the stages? Work them out with your partners. Here are some phrases that may be useful.

is/are peeled • is/are cut • is/are sliced •
is/are boiled • is/are fried • is/are grilled •
is/are roasted • is/are baked •
is/are stirred • is/are added • is/are served

C Using this grammar in a new situation

Work in groups of three. Do you know the answers?

A European Food Quiz

1 In which European country is haggis made?
2 What is haggis made of?
3 Where in Europe is the best beer brewed?
4 How many courses are served in a traditional German Sunday lunch?
5 In a French restaurant which is eaten first, cheese or dessert?

Now make three more questions like this.
Can your partners answer them?

Summary

Reading
– What does INTEX manufacture?
– It has centres in England, Wales, France – and which other countries?
– Its products are used in clothing, transport, flooring – and what else?

Pronunciation w, th, b, d, g, r, t, dr, tr
– Remember the way these sounds are produced at the beginning of a word, in the middle of a word, at the end of a word.
– Remember the different ways of pronouncing: th and r.

Learning Tip
English words do not always sound the way they are spelled. It is easier to learn and check the pronunciation of new words if you know how to read phonetic script. Most English-English dictionaries have the words written in normal script and then in phonetic script e. g. speak [spiːk]. *You can find a key to the phonetic symbols on the bookmarker of this Course Book.*

Grammar the passive
– The pasta is added to the boiling water.
– The vegetables are sliced.
– The best beer in Europe is brewed in . . . .

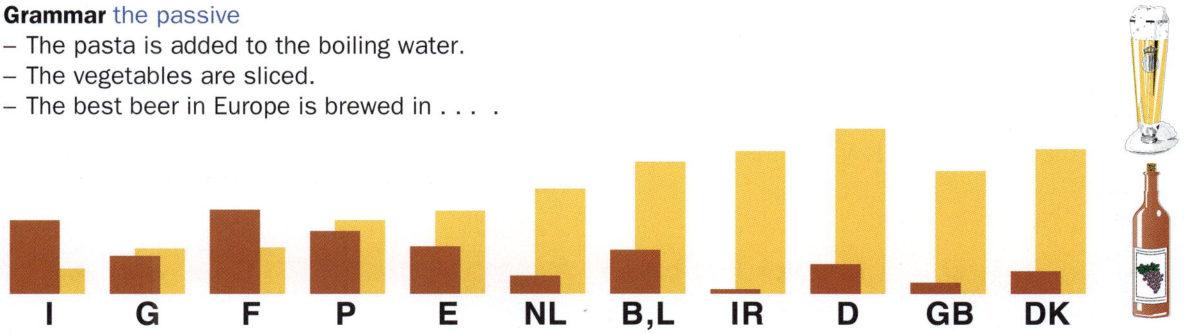

Review

This module is to help you:
★ to remember what you have covered in this session.
★ to evaluate your performance and progress.
★ to identify and remember some vocabulary and language of interest to you.

Work on your own at home after the session.

1 Fill in the Record Chart on page 51.
Look through the Summary at the top of this page and remember the activities you did in class.

2 Write down here:
Three key words you want to remember.

____________ ____________ ____________

Three key phrases or structures you want to remember.

____________ ____________ ____________

Reading module

In this module you are going to:
- ★ meet one of the characters from English for Europe.
- ★ practise making predictions about the content of a text.
- ★ practise looking for specific information in a text.

Ana Vasquez is a 28-year old Spaniard who moved to Brussels last year to work for INTEX, a textile import-export firm.

A Prediction

Work on your own, then compare your predictions with a partner's.

1 Ana comes from Spain. What do you think she finds better about living in Belgium?
2 What disadvantages do you think she finds?

B Checking Predictions

English is the working language of INTEX and here is an article about Ana from their in-company newspaper. Read the first two sections. Were your predictions right?

Work on your own, then check your findings with a partner.

Ana Vasquez came from Barcelona to join us at INTEX last year. She is working in the marketing department and is married to a Belgian architect. We asked her about her impressions of life here in Brussels.

What is the advantage of living in Belgium?
Strangely enough, the fact that Belgium is a small country that is culturally divided. It is probably easier to live here than in countries like Britain, France or Germany. Probably foreigners feel more foreign there. It's not that Belgians are particularly open, but this is a country where everyone is forced to make an effort to speak or at least understand some other languages.

What about drawbacks?
They are a bit colder than Spaniards. For example they are less spontaneously friendly. It is harder to meet Belgians, but once you do they are more willing to open up. They invite you to their homes and go out of their way for you. This is not necessarily true in Spain.

What would you like to take with you when you go to Spain?
Pastry, definitely. Spain has good pastries, but they tend to be a bit heavy.

And what would you like to bring back?
The weather! In Spain it is so fantastic to be able to spend time outdoors. After the evening meal it's not uncommon to see whole families going out for a stroll – at least in the smaller towns. It's just a way of stretching the day.

Do you prefer Brussels or Barcelona as a city?
Well, I sometimes think that Barcelona has all the disadvantages of a big city. It is big, noisy and aggressive. But it is hard to go out and catch a movie or a show – unless you are willing to spend hours on the underground. These things are definitely much easier to do in Brussels, which is smaller and has more to offer on that level.

And what about Belgian bureaucracy?
Spain is pretty complicated as well, you know! When I got married, I had to get my birth certificate from Barcelona. That was quite a problem. But I have had problems here too. What often happens is that you don't have all the information you need to get your papers. So you have to be patient and go back a few times.

What cheers you up on your way to work?
Trees. They are much bigger here than the ones you find in Barcelona. Greenery is very nice. There are lovely parks in Barcelona but they are so well-tended that you can't walk on the grass. That's a shame.

Could you see yourself working anywhere else?
I suppose we could leave, but not necessarily to Spain. London, perhaps – but it is difficult living there. Or maybe Italy. But at the moment I am very happy here.

C Looking for specific information

Work on your own, then check your findings with a partner.

From the information given in the text:
★ name two specific things that Ana prefers in Belgium.
★ add one thing she prefers in Spain.
★ find one thing that is a problem in both countries.

Grammar module the future continuous

In this module you are going to:
★ look at some examples of this grammar point in action.
★ practise using this grammar to talk about your future plans.
★ practise using this grammar in descriptions of other people's plans.

A Grammar in action

Ana Vasquez's secretary has prepared this memo for her.
Look at the information.

MEMO

To: *Ana Vasquez*
From: *Antje Miedema*
Date: *March 2nd*

Travel Arrangements

In connection with the meeting on Friday, the following travel arrangements have been made:

Pablo Gonzales will be arriving on IB 790 from Madrid at 08.45.
Maria Cellini will be coming on AZ 752 from Milan due in at 08.55.
Bruce Page will be catching a flight from Birmingham. Not sure of the flight number but it is due in at 09.05.
Pierre Dutronc won't be leaving Paris until 10.00. Details will be confirmed.

B Using this grammar in your situation

Work in a small group. Tell one another.

1 What you will be having for dinner tomorrow.
2 Where you will be going for your holidays this year.
3 What you will be doing after the class.
4 Where you will be living in ten years time.
5 How long you will be following this course.

C Using this grammar in new situations

Work in groups of three. Put the right form of the verb in the passages.

Do you remember *Sandra*, *Heather* and *Idris* who told you about their impressions of Europe? Here they are talking about their holiday plans for next year.

What about you? What are your plans?

Heather I'll be going to Spain. I'll be (spend) __________ the first week near the sea and then I'll (hire) __________ a car and I (drive) __________ into the mountains.

Idris I'll (visit) ____________ some friends in Germany. They live near Hamburg so we'll (see) __________ the sights of the city. I hope we (eat) __________ lots of local cakes and drinking lots of local beer as well.

Sandra I won't be (go) __________ abroad. My husband and I will (go) __________ to visit our children. We (spend) __________ the first week with my son and his family in Scotland and then we (catch) __________ the train to London to spend a week with my daughter.

Writing module

In this module you are going to practise writing descriptions of people in terms of:

- ★ height.
- ★ hair.
- ★ age.
- ★ clothes.

A Meeting visitors

Work alone.

Ana Vasquez has asked her secretary, Antje, to meet the visitors who are arriving at the airport. To help Antje to recognise them, Ana has prepared some descriptions. Here is the first one she has done:

Pablo Gonzales is about 28 and quite tall – about 1.80m. He has short dark hair and a moustache. He usually wears casual clothes and hates wearing a tie.

Now write notes for Antje about the other visitors who are coming:

a Maria Cellini/in her mid thirties/fairly tall 1.70m/long black hair/slim/dresses very elegantly/lot of jewellery.
b Bruce Page/early fifties/not very tall 1.60m/rather overweight/grey hair going bald/very old brown briefcase.
c Pierre Dutronc/35/1.80m/dark hair/round black glasses/small, neat beard.

B Comparing descriptions

Work in groups of three.

Compare the descriptions you have made.

C Describing groups

Work in groups of three.

Look at the photographs of the two groups of people.

What do the people in each group have in common? What makes each member of the group different?

Here is a description of one of the groups. Write a similar description of the other one.

There are three people in the group. They are all men and they are sitting on a bench, perhaps in a park. They are all senior citizens. Two of them are wearing glasses, the other one has his glasses in the pocket of his T-shirt. One of the men wearing glasses is also wearing a white cap.

These words might help you.

umbrella • blonde • auburn • dress • skirt • blouse • striped shirt • grey check trousers

Summary

Reading
– Name two specific things that Ana prefers in Belgium.
– Add one thing she prefers in Spain.
– Remember one thing that is a problem in both countries.

Grammar the future continuous
– Pablo Gonzales will be arriving on IB 790 from Madrid at 08.45.
– What will you be having for dinner tomorrow?
– I won't be going abroad.

Learning Tip
Some people find that music helps them to remember words. Try and fit as many of the sentences in the grammar module to the music of the song "She'll be coming round the mountain when she comes", e.g.
"We'll be spending the first week with our son;
We'll be spending the first week with our son;
We'll be spending the first week,
Spending the first week,
Spending the first week with our son."

Writing
– He is quite tall/not very tall.
– She is about 28/in her mid thirties. He is in his early fifties.
– He has short dark hair and a moustache./He has grey hair./ He is going bald./He has a small, neat beard.
– She is slim. He is rather overweight.
– She dresses very elegantly. He usually wears casual clothes.

Review

This review is to help you:
★ to remember what you have covered in this session.
★ to evaluate your performance and progress.
★ to identify and remember some vocabulary and language of interest to you.

Work on your own at home after the session.

1 Fill in the Record Chart on page 51. Look through the Summary at the top of these page and remember the activities you did in class.

2 Write down here:
Three key words you want to remember.

__________ __________ __________

Three key phrases or structures you want to remember.

__________ __________ __________

Listening module

In this module you are going to listen to a short talk and:
- identify specific words missing from a set of notes.
- identify the order in which certain points are made.
- expand a set of notes.

A Missing words

Work on your own.

Ana Vasquez is re-designing her company's publicity brochure. She is presenting a report on this project at a meeting in Brussels to a group of directors from other departments of the company in other European countries.

Before you listen to Ana's presentation, look at the rough notes she made when she started preparing her talk. Check any words you do not understand in an English-English dictionary.

By the time Ana gave her presentation at the meeting, she had added the information that was missing in her notes. Listen to the first part of the presentation and write the missing information in the spaces in Ana's notes.

New Brochure: Progress Report

Part 1 – Research

Old brochure 198___: old-fashioned/incorrect information
Questionnaire: Three groups

1 every employee in the company
2 ______ questionnaires to each European centre
3 to each of our current clients ______ questionnaires sent out.

Results
___% – not enough pictures
70% – text too technical
___% – not native-speakers/text too difficult
___% – picture of company chairman/negative image

60% – positive aspects:
- does not create pollution
- high quality, safe, inexpensive products
- latest technology.

B First, second, third, . . .

Work on your own.

In the second part of her presentation, Ana puts forward her five main proposals for the new company brochure. Check the meaning of any words in the notes that you do not understand.

As you listen to the second part of the cassette, write the numbers 1 to 5 next to the proposals to show the order in which Ana says them.

Part 2 – Proposals

reduce technical information	________
increase number of pictures	________
profiles of company employees	________
graphic design consultants	________
update information about company locations	________

C What is missing?

Work in a small group.

Now listen to the whole presentation again. As you listen, write down any important information which is not included in the notes above. Compare your notes with your partners' notes.

Vocabulary module

In this module you are going to:

- ★ revise some nationality adjectives you already know and learn some new ones.
- ★ re-construct a text about work using words you have checked in the dictionary.

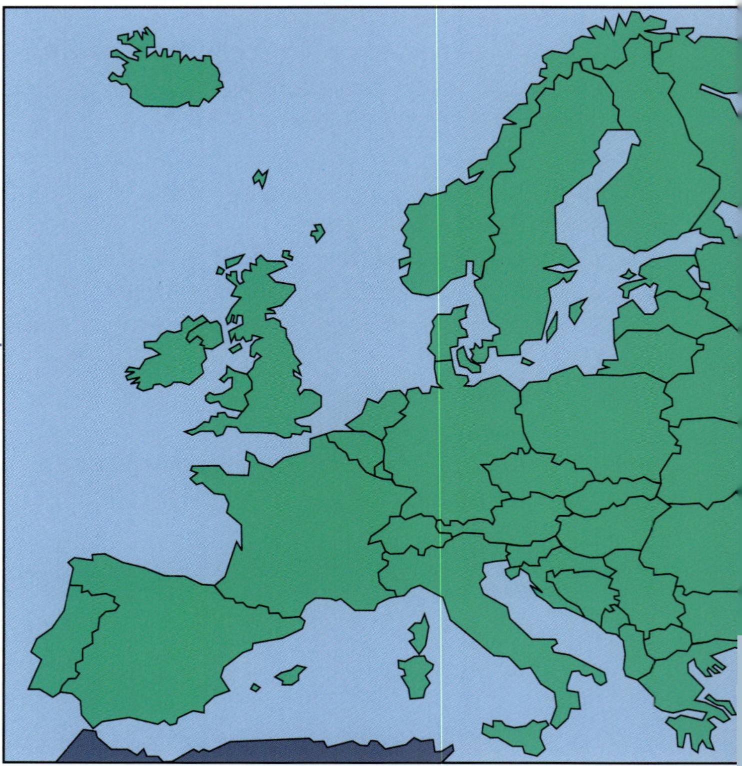

A European countries and nationality adjectives

Work on your own and with a partner.

Look at the map of Europe and match the numbers on the map with the names of the countries on page 27.

Switzerland • Austria • Italy • Denmark • Norway • Spain • The Netherlands • Poland • Hungary • Portugal • France • Ireland • Wales • Belgium

1 ______________ 2 ______________ 3 ______________
4 ______________ 5 ______________ 6 ______________
7 ______________ 8 ______________ 9 ______________
10 ______________ 11 ______________ 12 ______________
13 ______________ 14 ______________

Check your answer with a partner.

Below are the adjectives used to describe the people and things which come from these countries. The letters in each word are jumbled. Re-write them in their correct form.

shinDa	______________	sleWh	______________	gleniaB	______________
steeroguPu	______________	sliPho	______________	shirl	______________
grunaHina	______________	chernF	______________	cthuD	______________
shinSap	______________	nlliailta	______________	growNenia	______________
sSsiw	______________	raAnistu	______________		

B Applying for a job

Work on your own or with a partner.

Here is a group of words connected with getting a new job. Check the meaning of any words that are new to you in your English-English dictionary, then use them to fill the gaps in the following text.

P. A. to Sales Director of INTEX UK Ltd based in Gloucester.
Applicants should:

– have at least 5 years' experience as a P. A.
– be able to use their own initiative.
– be competent users of latest versions of Word and Microsoft Windows.
– be prepared to travel to overseas conferences.
– have a clean driving licence.

Salary by negotiation. Company pension scheme and health insurance.
Apply in writing with CV to:
Tim Bromley, Personnel Officer, INTEX UK Limited,
Ermin Street, GLOUCESTER GL3 4HP.

c. v. [curriculum vitae] •
satisfied • offer • apply • accept • joining • sales manager • qualifications • interview • advertisement • p. a. [personal assistant] • application • branch

Maggie wasn't really ______________ with her job. Last Friday she saw an ______________ for a job as ______________ to the ______________ in the local ______________ of an international textile firm. She wrote a letter of ______________ and sent it off with a copy of her ______________ on Saturday morning. The following week, she got a letter from the company inviting her to attend an ______________ . She was interviewed by the sales manager and the personnel manager. They asked her a lot of questions about her previous work experience and her ______________ ; they also asked her why she had decided to ______________ for the job. The following week she got a letter from the personnel officer telling her that her application had been successful and that they would like to ______________ her the job. She wrote another letter to say that she was happy to ______________ their offer and that she was looking forward to ______________ the company.

C Looking up the different noun, verb and adjective forms of a word

Work alone.

Now you have discovered the meaning of these words:

interview • accept • advertisement • apply • qualifications

Try and find the different forms of the word when it is used as a *noun*, a *verb*, and an *adjective*. Some words are not used in all the forms.

noun	*verb*	*adjective*
	to accept	
advertisement		
	to apply	
	to interview	
qualifications		

Grammar module the present simple and the present continuous

In this module you are going to:

- ★ look at some examples of this grammar point in action.
- ★ practise using this grammar to talk about your town or city.
- ★ practise using this grammar to talk about some of the characters from English for Europe.

A Grammar in action

Look at this information about Ana Vasquez's presentation to the group of INTEX directors.

1 She identified the four best features of the company.
- It does not create pollution.
- It provides good working conditions.
- It produces high quality products.
- It uses the latest technology.

2 She described what she is doing in her new brochure.
- She is updating the information about the company's locations in Europe.
- She is reducing the amount of technical information.
- She is employing graphic design consultants.
- She is increasing the human interest.

B Using this grammar in your situation

Work in a small group.

1 What do you think are the three best features of your town or city?
2 What is your town or city doing:
   • to improve the quality of life for local inhabitants?
   • to protect the local environment?
3 What opportunities are there locally to practise your English outside class?

C Using this grammar in new situations

Work in a group of three.

Put the verb in the right form – simple or continuous.

1 Pierre Dutronc (live) ____________________ just outside Paris. He has no plans to move.
2 Ana Vasquez and her husband (live) ____________________ in Brussels at the moment but they are thinking about moving later.
3 Bruce Page (work) ____________________ for INTEX in England. He would be happy to work for them until he retires.
4 Antje Miedema (work) ____________________ as Ana's secretary. Next year she will be leaving to go to America with her boyfriend.
5 Maria Cellini (drive) ____________________ every day from her home to the factory in Como.
6 She (want) ____________________ to get a new car as soon as she can afford one.
7 She (try) ____________________ to save up to buy one.

What about you?

Summary

Listening
– Identifying specific words missing from a set of notes.
  When was the old brochure produced?
– Identifying the order in which certain points are made.
  What is Ana's first proposal for the new brochure?
– Expanding a set of notes.
  What information was on the tape but was not in the notes?

Vocabulary
– The names of countries. How many of them can you remember. There were fourteen.
– Applying for a job: advertisement • to send off a letter of application • curriculum vitae (c. v.) • to attend an interview • she was interviewed by . . . • her previous experience • her qualifications • to offer her the job

Learning Tip
Look up the different noun, verb and adjective forms of every new word you learn and you will increase your own personal vocabulary quickly and with little extra effort.

Grammar the present simple and the present continuous
– INTEX provides good working conditions.
– It does not create pollution.
– Pierre Dutronc lives just outside Paris.
– Ana is updating the information about the company's locations in Europe.
– What is your town doing to protect the local environment?
– Ana and her husband are living in Brussels at the moment.

Review

Work on your own at home after the session.

1 Fill in the Record Chart on page 51. Look through the Summary at the top of this page and remember the activities you did in class.

2 Write down here:
Three key words you want to remember.

____________ ____________ ____________

Three key phrases or structures you want to remember.

____________ ____________ ____________

Grammar module wouldn't/ought to/had better

In this module you are going to:
- ★ look at some examples of this grammar point in action.
- ★ practise using this grammar to give and get advice about plans.
- ★ practise using this grammar to give advice to someone who is not feeling well.

A Grammar in action

After her presentation, Ana gets this memo from the Managing Director of INTEX.
Look at the memo and Ana's comment.

INTEX
MEMO

From the Office of the Managing Director

Dear Ana
I have heard about your plans for a new brochure. I think this is an excellent idea.
1. I wouldn't use the same firm of graphic designers we used last time. They are rather old-fashioned.
2. You ought to get first-hand information about the different company locations as well as the people you are going to profile. I think you ought to plan visits to all of them.

Yours
F. Lagerberg

I'd better not use Joseph Designs again. And I'd better start making some travel plans!

B Using this grammar in your situation

Work in small groups.

Take turns. Tell your partners about a plan you have. One will secretly give you some advice about what to do or what not to do. See if your other partner agrees.

C Using this grammar in a new situation

Work with a partner.

Your partner is feeling ill. What advice can you give him/her?

I've got a sore throat.
I've got a headache.
I've got a temperature.
I've got stomach ache.
I feel sick.
I think I've eaten too much.
I've got a terrible hangover.

And what about you?
What advice do you have for yourself at the moment?

I'd better . . . .
I'd better not . . . .

Interaction module

In this module you are going to:
★ listen to Ana Vasquez arranging a meeting with Yves Lanson in Lyon.
★ make a note of your plans for the next fortnight.
★ discuss a group social evening and try and arrange a convenient evening for the whole group to meet.

A Arranging a meeting

Work on your own.

Listen to Ana Vasquez arranging a business meeting with Yves Lanson in Lyon. Pay special attention to the way they both react.

- Making suggestions about a possible time for the meeting.
  How about the first week in March?
  What about the week after that?

- Saying that a particular time is not convenient.
  That week is no good for me . . .
  I can't manage that week . . .

- Saying that a particular time is convenient.
  Yes, that is a possibility.
  The following week would be all right.
  Yes, that suits me fine.

- The words in blue can be replaced by a reference to a month, date, day of the week or a time.
  The following week would be all right.
  June would be all right.
  The 27th would be all right.
  Wednesday would be all right.
  Half past six would be all right.

B Make a note of your plans

Work on your own.

Look at the pages from a diary below. Start with today and fill in the dates for the next fortnight. Now write down what you are planning to do in the evenings for the next two weeks.

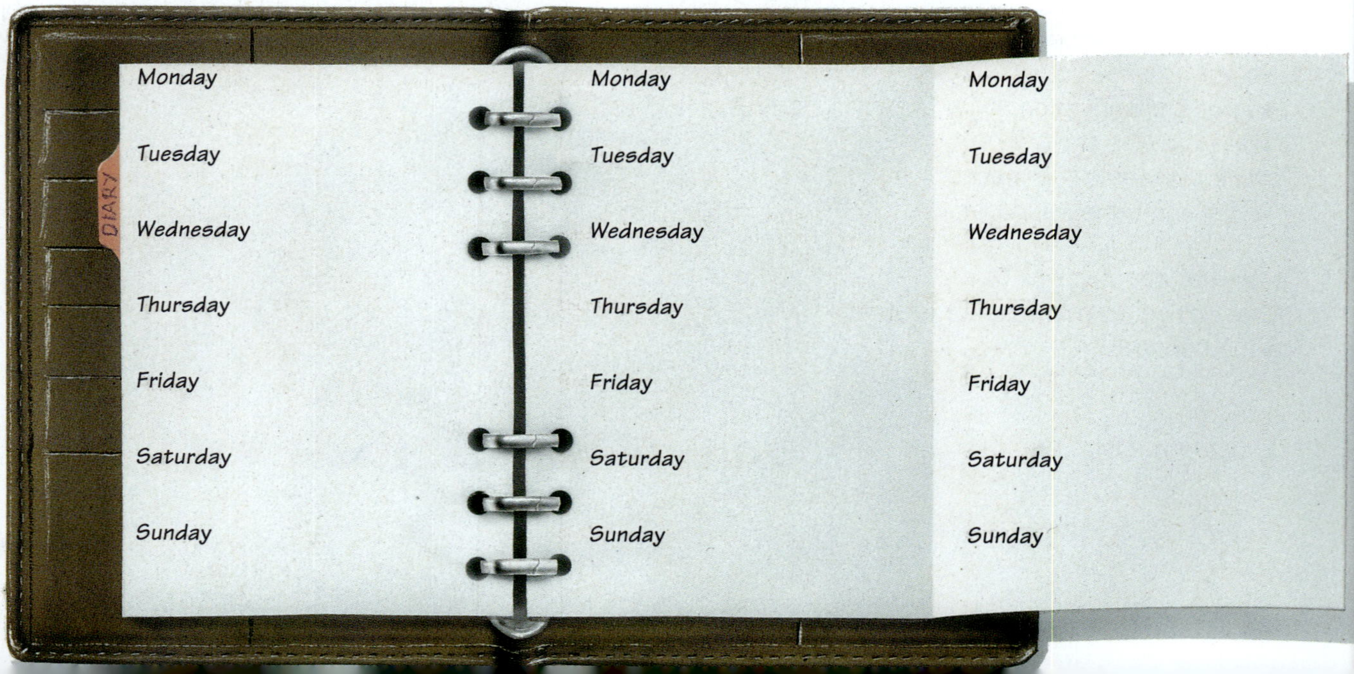

C Arranging a date

Work with a partner.

You have been studying English with the people in your class for some time now and you decide that it would be a good idea to arrange some kind of social evening for the whole group.

Find out which evenings your partner is free during the next two weeks and make a note of dates when you are both free.

D Arranging a date

Work in a group of three.

Make a group with two new people. Find a date when you all (and your partners from **C**) are free.

Reading module

In this module you are going to:
★ scan read a newspaper article for specific information.
★ re-locate that information in a different kind of text.
★ deduce information from the text.

A Looking for information

Work on your own, then in a group of three.

Crossing the Channel

Before the Channel Tunnel between England and France opened in 1994, each of the companies which operated the rail, sea and air links between England and mainland Europe tried to persuade more passengers to use their services by cutting the price of their fares. Look at this newspaper article that appeared in 1994; do not try and understand every word of the text.

Read the article in order to locate:

a the names of the companies which operate the rail, sea and air links between England and mainland Europe.
b the cost of travelling.
c how long the journey takes using different types of transport.

Mark the location of this information in the text.

Compare your answers with two partners.

5

THE EUROPEAN

EUROPEAN NEWSPAPER OF THE YEAR UK 75p

No 192 14 - 20 January 1994

Channel Tunnel is set to start a cut-price fares war

Askold Krushelnycky in London

EUROPEAN travellers will reap the rewards of a price war among rail, ferry and airlines that will mean cheaper fares when the Channel Tunnel begins operating.

Eurotunnel startled competitors and potential customer by unveiling rail ticket prices which in many cases are dearer than ferry fares. Return prices for a car travelling between England and France – regardless of the number of passengers – range from £220 to £310 (Ffr 2,720), depending on the time of year.

Ferry operators breathed a deep sigh of relief, and the price of Eurotunnel shares fell in Paris and London by 3.2 per cent.

But travel industry experts predict that Eurotunnel will drop some of its prices, to achieve its target to control half the market within a few years. And they expect lively competition between airlines and Eurostar, the tunnel's rail passenger service, when it begins operations later in the summer. Eurotunnel's commercial director, Christopher Garnett, expects Eurotunnel to carry eight million cars and 4.5 million coach passengers a year by 1996.

He forecasts that the very existence of the link will create a further one million passengers a year. The opening of the £10 billion 50 km tunnel is due in March for freight and May for passengers. Coaches will be taken from 5 September.

The Queen and President Mitterand will officially open the tunnel on 6 May. Like ferry prices, Eurotunnel fares for Le Shuttle – the service which will carry cars on double-decker rail wagons and coaches on single-deckers – will vary according to the season. But prices will remain the same no matter what time of day travellers want to make the crossings.

At peak summer weekends and holidays, a car load of people travelling between Folkestone and Calais can save £10 (Ffr 88) over typical return ferry fares charged be P&O or Stena Sealink. At peak periods, hovercraft fares will generally be more expensive than Le Shuttle, but Hoverspeed claims its total journey time will be twenty minutes shorter.

When Eurostar – owned ar
operated by the French, Be
gian and British national rai
ways – begins services, po
sibly in June, passengers wi
be able to travel betwee
Paris or Brussels and Londo
in around three hours.

The main rivals for the
journeys will be the airline
and observers predict fierc
competition.

Airline passengers betwee
London and Paris pay abo
£90 (Ffr 800) for the chea
est available return trip (£2
for business class). Brussel
to-London return tickets b
gin at around £100 (£304
business class).

The passenger trains (n
cars will be taken) will o
erate from the Gare du No
in Paris, Brussels Midi, ar
Waterloo Station London.

BY TUNNEL: Calais-Dover
Le Shuttle cars or coaches on trains.
Best crossing time: 65 minutes.
Fares: per car, including unlimited passengers, from £220 (Ffr 1,936) to £310 (Ffr 2,728) return, depending on season.
Eurostar train passengers.
Best time: Paris-London, 3 hours; Brussels-London, 3hr 10min.
No fares yet available.

BY AIR: Best time: 4 hours, including check-in
Brussels-London (BA & Sabena).
Fares: £127 (Bfr 6,985) to £304 (Bfr 16,720) return
Paris-London (BA & Air France)
£90 (Ffr 792) to £270 (Ffr 2,376) return.

BY SEA: Calais-Dover
P & O Ferry: Best crossing time 105 minutes.
Fares: per car, including unlimited passengers, from £139 (Ffr 1,200) t
£289 (Ffr 2,540) return, depending on season.
Sealink Ferry: Best crossing time: 105 minutes.
Fares: per car, including unlimited passengers, from £126 (Ffr 1,109) t
£220 (Ffr 1,936) return, but with £50 supplement at some peak periods
Hoverspeed: Best crossing time: 45 minutes.
Fares: per car, with two adults and three children, £142
(Ffr 1,250) to £333 (Ffr 2,930) return.

B Using information

Work in groups of three.

Each member of the group chooses one of the three texts below and fills in the missing information.

BY TUNNEL: Calais – Dover
________ *1:* cars or coaches on trains.
Best crossing time: 65 minutes
Fares: per car, including unlimited passengers, from (£) ________ 2 (Ffr 1,936) to £ ________ 3 (Ffr ____ 4) return depending on season.
________ *5:* train passengers.
Best times: Paris – London, 3 hours; Brussels – London 3hr 10min. No fares yet available.

BY AIR: Best time: 4 hours including check-in ________ 1 – London (BA and Sabena).
Fares: £127 (Bfr 6,985) to £ ________ 2 (Bfr 16,720) return
Paris – London (BA and Air France) £ ________ 3 (Ffr ________ 4) to £ ________ 5 (Ffr 2,376) return.

BY SEA: Calais – Dover
P&O Ferry: Best crossing time: 105 minutes.
Fares, per car including unlimited passengers, from £ ________ 1 (Ffr 1,200) to £289 (Ffr 2,540) return depending on season.
________ *2* ***Ferry: Best crossing time:*** 105 minutes.
Fares: per car, including unlimited passengers, from £ ________ 3 (Ffr 1,109) to £220 (Ffr ________ 4) return, but with £50 supplement at some peak periods.
________ *5:* ***Best crossing time:*** 45 minutes.
Fares: per car, with two adults and three children, £142 (Ffr 1,250) to £333 (Ffr 2,930) return.

C Using the text to make decisions

Work in groups of three.

Check the information that the other two people in your group have found. Using this information decide:

1 Which is the fastest way to travel from London to Paris?
2 Which is the fastest way to get from Calais to Dover?
3 Which is the cheapest way to take your car from England to France?
4 Which is the cheapest way for a family of three adults and two children to travel from France to England?

Summary

Grammar wouldn't/ought to/had better
- I wouldn't use the same firm again.
- I think you ought to plan visits to all the European factories.
- I'd better not use that firm again.
- I'd better start making travel plans.

Interaction
- How about the first week in March?
- What about the week after that?
- That week is no good for me.
- I can't manage that week.
- Yes, that is a possibility.
- The following week would be all right.
- Yes, that suits me fine.

Learning Tip
Record your own voice on an audio cassette. Record the new words and phrases in the summary at the end of each session; this will give you extra speaking practice, help you to memorise the new words and phrases and increase your confidence the next time you use them in a real conversation.

Reading
- Scan reading a newspaper article for specific information.
- Using that information in a different kind of text.
- Using the text to make decisions.
- Which is the fastest way to travel from London to Paris?
- Which is the fastest way to get from Calais to Dover?
- Which is the cheapest way to take your car from England to France?
- Which is the cheapest way for a family of three adults and two children to travel from France to England?

Review

Work on your own at home after the session.

1 Fill in the Record Chart on page 51. Look through the Summary at the top of this page and remember the activities you did in class.

2 Write down here:
Three key words you want to remember.

____________ ____________ ____________

Three key phrases or structures you want to remember.

____________ ____________ ____________

6 Travel

Pronunciation module

In this module you are going to:

★ Listen to and repeat words containing the sound /æ/ as in HAT and /e/ as in HEAD.
★ Identify the number of syllables in different words.
★ Identify stressed and unstressed syllables in different words.

A Focus on the sounds /æ/ and /e/

Work on your own, then with a partner.

Listen to the following words first read by a native speaker of English and then by a non-native speaker of English. The pronunciation is a little different, but both people are easy to understand. One the tape the pairs of words are sometimes said in reverse order. Which word is first and which is second? Write the number 1 or 2 next to the appropriate word. Check your answers with a partner.

Pair a	BAD	______	BED	______
Pair b	SAD	______	SAID	______
Pair c	MAN	______	MEN	______
Pair d	HAD	______	HEAD	______
Pair e	DAD	______	DEAD	______
Pair f	SAT	______	SET	______
Pair g	PAN	______	PEN	______

Now listen to the tape again and repeat the words.

B Syllables

Work on your own, then with a partner.

When you say the word **HOVERCRAFT** you can hear that it is divided into three different sound sections like this: **HO-VER-CRAFT**. Each of these sound sections is called a "syllable".
You are going to hear a list of six words. You will hear each word twice. Make a note of how many syllables there are in each word.

1	______	2	______
3	______	4	______
5	______	6	______

Check your answer with a partner.

C Stressed and unstressed syllables

Work on your own and with a partner.

In all English words there is at least one syllable which is pronounced louder than the other syllables. In the word **HO-VER-CRAFT**, the first syllable is louder than the other two syllables. The louder syllable is called a "stressed syllable".
One way of showing the relationship between the stressed and unstressed syllables in a word is to use large and small circles, for example:
O-o-o = **HO-VER-CRAFT**. The large and small circles represent the stress pattern of the word.
Write each word next to the correct stress pattern.

TERMINAL • RETURN • LOCOMOTIVE • INFORMATION • FERRY • BICYCLE

1 **O-o-o** ____________ 2 **o-o-O-o** ____________
3 **o-O** ____________ 4 **O-o-o** ____________
5 **O-o** ____________ 6 **o-o-O-o** ____________

Check your answers with your partner.

Grammar module

the past simple and present perfect simple

In this module you are going to:
- ★ look at some examples of this grammar point in action.
- ★ practise using this grammar to talk about recent events.
- ★ practise using this grammar to describe where people live.

A Grammar in action

Ana Vasquez has asked her secretary, Antje Miedema, to start making some travel arrangements for her visits.

Look at this note she leaves for Antje.

Here are a few things to remember about the arrangements
1 Have you spoken to Alison Steadman in Gloucester? I've never been to Gloucester before so I'll need good directions.
2 I've already booked my flight to Milan. Maria Cellini has arranged it for me.
3 I spoke to Mart Wekker in Rozenburg last week and he promised to send some background information on the Dutch factories. Has it arrived yet?
4 Where have you put the tickets for my flight to Lyon? I can't find them in the file.
Thanks

B Using this grammar in your situation

Work on your own, then in small groups.

What happpened last week? In politics, in sport or in any other area – in your town/city, in your country or in Europe?

Make a list and then compare your list with your partners'.

Look at some of the sentences on your lists. Can you add a sentence saying what has happened as a result?

Last week the Government increased the tax on petrol. So I have decided to buy a smaller car.

C Using this grammar in new situations

Work in a group of three.

Past simple or present perfect?

Ana and her husband (buy) ___________ their house last year. When they (move) ___________ in they (re-decorate) ___________ the bedroom and (buy) ___________ some new equipment for the kitchen but since then they (be) ___________ too busy to do anything else. They want to clean out the cellar to store wine there, but they (not find) ___________ the time yet.

After a long search Antje and her boyfriend (now find) ___________ a flat near the centre of Brussels which they (decide) ___________ to rent. Antje (not like) ___________ the flat where they (live) ___________ before because it (not be) ___________ big enough and it (take) ___________ too long to get into the centre of the city.

What about you? When did you move to the place where you live now?

Writing module

In this module you are going to practise:
- ★ making changes in a draft letter.
- ★ writing a letter to confirm arrangements.

A Correcting a draft

Work on your own, then with a partner.

Ana Vasquez has written to Alison Steadman in Gloucester. This is a draft of the letter which Antje Miedema has typed. Ana has marked some changes which she wants Antje to make.

Re-write the letter making the changes and then compare your version with a partner's.

Ms A Steadman
INTEX UK Ltd
Ermin St
Brockworth
Gloucester GL3 4HP
England

INTEX International
73, rue Archimède
B 1040 Bruxelles / Brussel
Tel (+ 32 2) 295 38 44
Fax (+ 32 2) 295 67 89

Dear Alison **Ms Steadman – I don't know her very well**

I am writing to confirm the arrangements for my visit to Gloucester. **say when: next week**
As you know I am working on a new publicity brochure for the INTEX Group, featuring background information on all the European locations of the Group, and profiles of some of the people who work in each centre.
I hope very much that you will be able to provide me with an insight into the centre in Gloucester, and that you will be kind enough to let me interview you in order to include a profile of you in the new brochure. **add something to say why we have chosen to profile Alison**
I shall be arriving on Tuesday evening next week at approximately **no, Wednesday** *6.30 p.m. and have reserved a room at the White Swan Hotel for Tuesday and Wednesday nights.* **no, Wednesday and Thursday** *Thank you for your invitation to have dinner at your home on Wednesday evening. I shall be bringing a car so perhaps you could leave directions to tell me how to get to your house. Could we discuss the programme for Wednesday over dinner?* **no, Thursday**
I have booked a ferry crossing for Friday evening, so I will have to leave at about 10.00 on Friday. **could be later say about 12.00**
Thank you for your help in making these arrangements. I look forward to seeing you next week.
With best wishes
Yours

Ana Vasquez
Marketing Co-ordinator **let's make it more formal to go with dear Ms Steadman. How about . . . yours sincerely**

B Writing a letter

Work on your own, then with a partner.

Draft a similar letter to:

Yves Lanson
INTEX France S. A.
47, rue Ferrandiere
Lyon 33 Cedex
France

Ana knows Yves quite well and so she writes a more informal letter.

Compare your letter with a partner's.

Summary

Pronunciation
- Sounds /æ/ as in hat and /e/ as in head.
- Stressed and unstressed syllables.
- Stress patterns.

Learning Tip
Check the stress pattern of the new words you learn in a dictionary. The syllable with the main stress is usually shown marked by the symbol ˈ in the phonetic transcription of the word. So the stress pattern O-o-o of the word beautiful, is indicated like this: /ˈbjuːtɪful/.

Grammar the past simple and the present perfect simple
- Last week the government increased the tax on petrol.
- They bought their flat two years ago.
- She didn't like the flat where they lived before.
- Have you spoken to Alison in Gloucester?
- I've never been to Gloucester before.
- I've already booked my flight to Milan.
- Has the information arrived yet?

Writing
- Remember the way the address is laid out.
- Remember the more formal and the more friendly forms of opening and closing:
  Dear Ana . . . With best wishes • Dear Mrs/Ms Steadman Yours sincerely •
  Dear Madam/Sir . . . Yours faithfully • I am writing to confirm . . . • As you know, . . . •
  I hope very much that . . . • I shall be arriving . . . • I look forward to seeing you

Review

Work on your own at home after the session.

1 Fill in the Record Chart on page 51. Look through the Summary at the top of this page and remember the activities you did in class.

2 Write down here:
Three key words you want to remember.

__________ __________ __________

Three key phrases or structures you want to remember.

__________ __________ __________

Reading module

In this module you are going to:

- ★ identify the source of three texts.
- ★ scan the newspaper text and identify specific information.
- ★ locate and collect information on specific topics from each of the texts.

A What sort of text is this?

Work on your own, then in a group of three.

These three texts come from a *Guide Book*, a *Newspaper* and a *Gazetteer* at the back of an atlas published in Britain. Decide which text (Text A, Text B, Text C) is which and write notes on the reasons for your decision. Compare your answers and your reasons with your partners.

Text A

LYON – MUSEUMS AND CHURCHES

Musée de l'Imprimérie et de la Banque – Rue Poulaillerie: The history of printing and banking.
Musée des Beaux Arts – Rue Constantine: Second largest collection of paintings and sculpture in France.
Musée Historique des Tissus et des Arts Décoratifs – Rue de la Charité: The history of textiles, particularly silk, and the decorative arts.
Cathédrale Saint Jean: cathedral church of the Primate of the Gauls situated in the old quarter of Lyon. Building began in the twelfth century. The marble at the base of the facade comes from the Forum of Trajan. Henri IV and Marie de Médicis were married here.
Saint Martin d'Ainay – Rue des Remparts d'Ainay: Romanesque church near the Perrache commercial centre.
Notre Dame de Fourvière: Romano-Byzantine basilica.
Fourvière: Hill to the west of the Saône where the Roman settlement of Lugdunum was located. The word Fourvière comes from the Latin words *forum vetus* meaning "old forum". Roman amphitheatre and Gallo-Roman architectural remains.

Text B

LYONS – [French spelling: Lyon] 45 47N 4 50E Second largest city in France; pop. 1.25 million approx.; capital of Rhône département at confluence of Rhône and Saône rivers; textile centre since XV century esp. silk; financial , legal and university centre; ancient Lugdunum taken by Romans 43 B.C.; Strong revolutionary tradition after 1793; industry: textiles, pharmaceutical products, synthetics, chemicals, machinery, printing. ■

Text C

THE EUROPEAN
CITY GUIDES

SITUATION
South-Eastern France, in the Rhône/Saône valley, 470 km from Paris, or two hours by TGV. 340 km from Marseille.

AROUND THE CITY
Extensive bus and underground train network: tickets Ffr 7, booklets of six Ffr 36. One ticket valid on whole network (incl funicular) for up to four trips in any one hour. Street parking is mostly metered. Car parks under the place Bellecour, place des Terreaux, and place de la République.

TRANSPORT
24 km from ***Satolas airport***, or approximately 25 minutes by taxi; cost Ffr 220, depending on time of day, minimum fare Ffr 25. Shuttle bus from Satolas to city centre every 20 minutes, 0600-2300 h, cost Ffr 40.

HOTELS
Cour des Loges, 2-4-6-8 rue du Boeuf, tel 78427575, fax 72409361: beautiful 14 – 17th century building.
La Tour Rose, 22 rue du Boeuf, tel 78372590, fax78422602: grew from its famous restaurant into a tiny, intimate hotel, furnished in silks

RESTAURANTS
Léon de Lyon, 1 rue Pleney, tel 78281133, a restaurant offering typical local cuisine; open Mon eves – Sat 2200h. ***Pierre Orsi***, 3 place Kleber, tel 78895768, for more typical local cuisine.

BARS
Try one of the many *bouchons* in the old town: these are small restaurants offering pure Lyonnais gastronomic delights and great convivality. ***Café des Fédérations***, 8 rue du Major Martin, tel 78282600; open Mon – Fri

SHOPPING
Place Bellecour des Terreaux, rue de la République, rue Herriot, Cours Vitton, for the best boutiques, and ***Centre Commercial de la Part-Dieu***, a mall with more than 280 shops near the Part-Dieu station. Shops open Tues-Sat 0900 – 1200 h, 1400 – 1900 h. Flea markets: ***Chemin de la Feyssine*** (17 – 19 rue Rougetde-l'Isle), open Sun 0600 – 1300 h, or ***rue Tita-Cols***, Sun 0730 – 1200 h, or the ***rue Auguste Comte*** for antiques.

AN HOUR TO SPARE
Roman splendour
Explore the *traboules* or alleys of the ***Old Town*** between the rue Saint-Jean, rue des Trois Maries and the quai Romain Rolland; visit the ***Institut Lumière***, dedicated to the film projector, 25 rue du Premier-Film, open Tues – Sun 1400 – 1800 h, or the ***Musée des Beaux-Arts***, France's second-largest fine arts museum; take the funicular up Fourvière hill for spectacular views and the ***Gallo-Roman Museum***, open Wed – Sun 0930 – 1200 h and 1400 – 1800 h, and the ***Roman Amphitheatre*** (*above*), the oldest in France.

WHEN YOU ARE THERE ***Lyon Poche*** a guide to what's on, is available at newsagent. Try Espace Gerson, 1 Place Gerson, tel 78279699 as a café. For theatre, try the newly refurbished Opéra, which reopens on 14 May, or one of the many ballets.
MAIN TRADE FAIRS AND EVENTS ***Bienale*** contemporary art exhibition 1/9 – 15/10; ***International Fair*** 27/3 – 5/4; ***Golf Open*** 1 – 4/4; ***Car show*** 2 – 10/10.
Exchange: Gare de Perrache, Gare de la Part-Dieu 0800 – 1900 h, seven days. Crédit Lyonnais, BNP, Crédit Nord 0900 – 1200 h, 1400 – 1600 h.
Thomas Cook representative: Via Voyages, 27/29 rue Ferrandiere, tel 78 42 18 42, fax 78 38 18 90, for leisure and business travel arrangements.

B Looking for information

Work on your own and check your answers with your partners.

Ana Vasquez has arranged to interview Yves Lanson, a technical operations manager at the INTEX Fibre Manufacture Centre in Lyon. She asks Antje Miedema, her secretary, to get her the *following* information about Lyon.

Use the newspaper text to make a note of the information Ana wants, and then compare your answers with your partners.

Antje, could you find out the following for my trip to Lyon – Is there an airport? How far from centre? What is the name of the main railway station? Where can I find out about theatre, concerts, films, etc? How far is it from Paris? Are there any trade fairs on in March? Where is the textile museum? Is there an underground in the city centre?
Thanks
Ana

C Locating and collecting information

Work in groups of three.

Scan the three texts and make a note of any information you can find on one of the following topics. (Choose a different topic from the other two people in your group.)

INDUSTRIES IN LYON – THE ROMANS IN LYON – THE GEOGRAPHY OF LYON

Swap information with your partners.

Interaction module

In this module you are going to:
- ★ listen to three people deciding which dish to choose from a menu.
- ★ plan a menu for a dinner party.
- ★ say which kinds of food you prefer.
- ★ say which kind of foods you don't like.
- ★ describe the ingredients in a particular dish.

A In a Restaurant

Work on your own.

Maria Cellini is in Brussels to visit a trade fair.
She is staying with her old friend, Ana Vasquez and her husband, Ralf Staelens. Maria invites both of them out to dinner, so they decide to go to a restaurant which has a traditional Belgian menu. Listen to the recording and fill in the missing words in the following sentences.

1 *I'm __________ to eggs.*
2 *I'm not very __________ on freshwater fish.*
3 *They're a __________ of shellfish.*
4 *I __________ mussels.*
5 *That __________ delicious.*
6 *I'm very __________ of mussels too.*

B Planning a menu for a dinner party

Work on your own.

You have invited six people to dinner at your home. Two of the people are from your class, but the other four are visitors from Canada. Plan the meal you would like to prepare for them. Include a starter, a main course and a dessert. Make sure you know the ingredients in each dish.

C Discussing your food preferences

Work in small groups.

Take turns to tell your partners about the menu you have planned for them. Explain what is in each dish. Find out whether they like it or not.

Grammar module participles and gerunds

In this module you are going to:

★ look at some examples of this grammar point in action.
★ practise using this grammar to talk about your feelings and reactions.
★ practise using this grammar to share some experiences with your partners.

A Grammar in action

Ana decides to hire a car for the trip to Gloucester. But she has never driven in England before so she is very interested in reading this leaflet.

Driving in Britain

Are you worried about driving in Britain? Don't be! Finding your way is very easy. And you will soon get used to driving on the left. Just remember these possible danger times.

1 Starting off after buying petrol. Remember to keep to the left!
2 Approaching a roundabout. Give way to traffic from the right.
3 Driving on the motorway. Remember to overtake only on the right.

Driving in Britain is simple and easy.

B Using this grammar in your situation

Have you ever driven in a foreign country? Or visited a place you didn't know? Or done something strange or exciting?

Work in small groups.

- What were you worried about before you did it?
- What were you looking forward to?
- What did you find difficult?
- What did you find easy?

Tell your partners. Have they done the same as you? Did they feel the same?

C Using this grammar in new situations

Work in a group of three.

Can you agree how to complete these sentences (use a verb with *-ing*).

1 The best thing about living here is ____________________ .
2 ____________________ is our teacher's greatest ambition.
3 It must be wonderful ____________________ .
4 ____________________ is not easy these days.
5 ____________________ was the biggest mistake the government ever made.

What about you?

Summary

Reading
- Identifying the source of three texts. What sort of texts were they? How did you decide which was which?
- Scanning the newspaper text and finding specific information. How far is Lyon from Paris? What is the name of the main railway station? What other information did Ana want?
- Locating and collecting information on specific topics from each of the texts. What did you find out about these topics? **Industries in Lyon • The Romans in Lyon • The Geography of Lyon**

Learning Tip

It is not necessary to understand the meaning of every single word in order to understand the general meaning of the text. None of the reading tasks in this book will ask you to do that. However, it is very important to be clear about your reason for reading a text before you start reading. Always read the instructions at least twice.

Interaction
- I'm allergic to eggs.
- I'm not very keen on freshwater fish.
- They're a kind of shellfish.
- I love mussels.
- How are they cooked?
- I'm very fond of mussels too.

Grammar participles and gerunds
- She is wondering about hiring a car.
- She is interested in reading this leaflet.
- Are you worried about driving in Britain?
- You will soon get used to driving on the left.
- Starting off after buying petrol } can be dangerous.
- Approaching a round about } can be dangerous.

Review

Work on your own at home after the session.

1 Fill in the Record Chart on page 51. Look through the Summary at the top of this page and remember the activities you did in class.

2 Write down here:
Three key words you want to remember.

____________________ ____________________ ____________________

Three key phrases or structures you want to remember.

____________________ ____________________ ____________________

Writing module

In this module you are going to practise:
- ★ writing a note of apology.
- ★ giving directions.

A A note of apology

Look at this note which Alison Steadman leaves at Ana's hotel in Gloucester.

Dear Ana Vasquez
Welcome to Gloucester. I hope you had a safe and pleasant journey.
I'm terribly sorry but we will have to change our arrangements for this evening. I have had to go unexpectedly to our factory in Pontypool for an urgent meeting this afternoon. I won't be back in Gloucester before 7.30.
I'm afraid I won't have time to prepare dinner at home, so I have booked us a table at my favourite Italian restaurant for 8.30. I hope you like Italian food!
I will pick you up here at the hotel at 8.15.
Sorry again for the change of plan.
With best wishes *Alison Steadman*

B Writing a note of apology

Work on your own, then with a partner.

Now write a similar note for a visitor to your town/city.

- How well do you know the visitor?
- Why have you had to change your plans?
- What new arrangements have you made?

Compare your note with your partner's.

C Writing directions

Work on your own, then with a partner.

Write some directions for your visitor telling him/her how to get to a well-known place in your town/city on foot from the hotel. Do not name the place. Can your partner work out where your directions are leading to?

Here are some phrases you might use.

turn left/right • go straight on • as far as • until you reach • cross • in front of you • to your left/right

Listening module

In this module you are going to:

- ★ listen to a set of directions and complete notes.
- ★ listen to a set of directions and take notes.
- ★ discuss the best route from Calais to Brussels.

Ana Vasquez is in Gloucester. She is having dinner with Alison Steadman and is already thinking about the return journey to Brussels. She asks Alison about the quickest way to get to Dover from the factory.

A Completing notes

Work on your own, then with a partner.

Listen to Alison explaining how to get from the INTEX centre in Gloucester to Dover. Complete this set of notes by writing in the missing information.

Route 1 – via Oxford

Turn _______ at main gates – top of steep _______ junction _______ to Andoversford. Turn right onto _______ to _______ at Andoversford. Join _______ at Wheatley. At Fulmer take _______ southbound. Join _______ at Sevenoaks then _______ at Maidstone. Continue on _______ (_______) until Dover.

Compare your answer with a partner's.

B Taking notes

Work on your own and check with a partner.

Listen to Alison describing the second route to Ana. Make notes like the ones in **A**.

Route 2 – via Swindon

The place names she mentions are: Andoversford/Cirencester/Datchet and Swindon.

C Deciding on the best route

Work in groups of three.

Ana decided to cross from Dover to Calais by car ferry. Look at the road map of northern France and Belgium. Discuss the best route from Calais to Brussels, then make a set of notes like the ones in **A** and **B** above.

Grammar module reported speech

In this module you are going to:

- ★ look at some examples of this grammar point in action.
- ★ practise using this grammar to tell the group about some predictions you make.
- ★ practise using this grammar in situations you invent.

A Grammar in action

When she gets back to her hotel, Ana writes a postcard to her husband.

Dear Ralf

I didn't know Gloucester was so big! I thought it was a quiet little place. What a surprise! I wonder if everybody has the same reaction as me? (I wonder if everybody has the same problems with the pronunciation as me??) I thought the cathedral was really beautiful. And I didn't know that there were docks here. So far from the sea!

See you on Friday night.

All my love

B Using this grammar in your situation

Work in small groups.

Nowadays many Europeans have moved to another European country. Decide with your group.

a In what European country can you find the highest number of citizens of other European countries?
b Where in Europe (outside Italy) do you think most Italians live?
c What nationality do you think is the largest group of Europeans who have moved to Spain?

Now check with the table on page 159. Were you right? Tell the rest of the class.

We thought that . . ./We didn't think that . . .

Is there any information in the table that surprises you?

C Using this grammar in new situations

Work in small groups.

Agree with your partners on how to complete these sentences.

1 I would like to find out when ________________ .
2 Before I started this course nobody warned me that ________________ .
3 Ana wants to ask Alison if ________________ .
4 I wonder how much ________________ .
5 I still don't know where ________________ .

What about you?

Summary

Writing

– Remember how Alison addressed Ana in the note: I hope you had a safe journey. • I'm terribly sorry but . . . • I'm afraid . . .
– Giving directions: Turn left / right . . . • Go straight on . . . as far as . . . until you reach . . . • Cross . . . • In front of you . . . • To your left/right . . .

Learning Tip

When you write in another language it is difficult not to translate one word at a time from your own language. If you do, you will probably make more mistakes. Always try and remember whole phrases in the foreign language and take examples of whole sentences from the text in the book. In this way you can be sure that the structure of the sentence is correct even if you get some words wrong.

Listening

– Listening to a set of directions and completing notes.
– Listening to a set of directions and taking notes.
– Discussing the best route from Calais to Brussels: Turn right at . . . • carry on until . . . • take the road signposted . . . • turn right onto the A40. • stay on the A40 until you get to . . . • the M25 interchange . . .

Grammar reported speech

– I didn't know it was so big.
– I thought it was a quiet little place.
– I wonder if everybody has the same reaction as me.
– She told me that she travels a lot.
– I found out that the company is expanding.

Review

Work on your own at home after the session.

1 Fill in the Record Chart on page 51.
Look through the Summary at the top of this page and remember the activities you did in class.

2 Write down here:
Three key words you want to remember:

__________ __________ __________

Three key phrases or structures you want to remember:

__________ __________ __________

Now that you have finished Block One, complete the Evalution Chart on page 52.

Record Chart Block One Sessions 1– 8

At the end of each session, record what you have done.

Session 1	Interaction ❏ Describing	Grammar ❏ must/mustn't needn't	Listening ❏ Europe
Session 2	Reading ❏ Intex	Pronunciation ❏ sounds	___________ ❏ passive
Session 3	___________ ❏ Ana Vasquez	___________ ❏ future continuous	Writing ❏ Describing
Session 4	___________ ❏ Ana's brochure	Vocabulary ❏ Nationalities	___________ ❏ present simple and continuous
Session 5	___________ ❏ wouldn't/ ought to	___________ ❏ Arrangements	___________ ❏ Crossing the Channel
Session 6	___________ ❏ stressed syllables	___________ ❏ past simple/ present perfect simple	___________ ❏ Letters
Session 7	___________ ❏ Lyons	___________ ❏ Food	___________ ❏ participles/ gerunds
Session 8	___________ ❏ Informal notes	___________ ❏ Directions	___________ ❏ reported speech

Evaluation Chart Block One Session 1– 8

Now that you have finished this block, think back over the work you have done in each area.

Which modules did you find easiest? Which hardest? Which areas do you need to concentrate on in your future work in English?

Fill in this chart to show how you feel about your performance in the seven areas covered by English for Europe. **This is your chart, for you.**

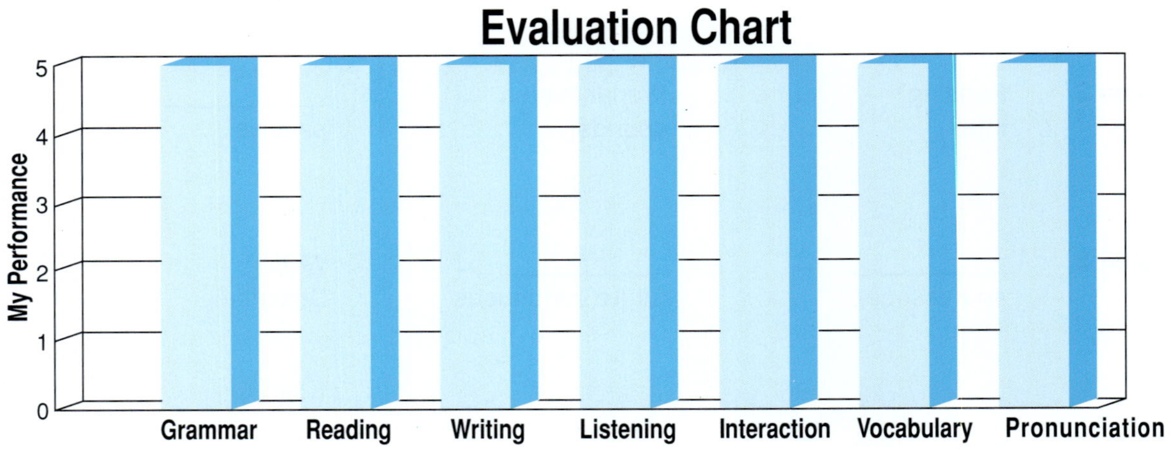

In each area, fill in the chart up to the number which you feel matches your performance.

Grammar

5 I knew all this already.
3 I knew some of this, but there was quite a lot of new material.
1 Nearly all the grammar we covered was new for me.

Reading & Listening

5 I understood everything.
3 I understood enough to answer the questions.
1 I didn't understand very much at all.

Writing

5 I can write what I want to say quite easily and without too many mistakes.
3 I know that my writing has some mistakes, but people can understand what I write.
1 I don't feel confident about writing in English. I find it hard.

Interaction

5 I can express what I want to say quite easily and without too many mistakes.
3 I know that when I speak English I make some mistakes but people can understand what I say.
1 I don't feel confident about speaking English. I find it hard.

Vocabulary

5 I knew all this already.
3 I knew some of this, but there was quite a lot of new material.
1 Nearly all the vocabulary we covered was new for me.

Pronunciation

5 I think my accent in English is quite good.
3 I find some sounds in English quite difficult, but people can understand me.
1 I have a lot of problems with English pronunciation.

Welcome to Block Two Sessions 9 – 16

This block consists of eight 90-minute sessions each of which is made up of two prescribed modules + one module selected from the Block Two Module Banks.

There is an overview (page 54) of what you will find in this block.

Each session in this block has one "free slot" into which a module from the Block Two Module Banks can be fitted.

This allows the group (learners and teacher) to shape each lesson to some extent according to their preferences.

Decisions about the module to be added in each session can be made during the lesson or in advance, according to the wishes and interests of the group.

It is not necessary to cover the modules from the Module Banks in the order in which they are printed.

Remember that follow-up material for each module is available in the Learner's Book

Prescribed Modules

9	**Grammar** conditionals 1	**Interaction** Asking & describing: weekend plans Warning:possible problems/stating alternatives
10	**Grammar** conditionals 2	**Writing** A description from notes
11	**Listening** Telephone messages	**Grammar** indirect questions and commands
12	**Grammar** past simple & past continuous past Perfect	**Reading** The Estonia disaster
13	**Grammar** quantifiers: countables & uncountables	**Interaction** Welcoming: Arranging the seating Offering/ accepting/declining Saying goodbye
14	**Grammar** present perfect & past perfect: simple & continuous	**Writing** Correcting a formal letter
15	**Reading** European stereotypes	**Grammar** causative use of ***have*** & ***get***
16	**Grammar** prepositions + adjectives/ verbs nouns + verb phrases	**Listening** Weather forecast

Module Banks

Grammar module conditionals

In this module you are going to:
- ★ look at some examples of this grammar point in action.
- ★ practise using this grammar to talk about problems.
- ★ practise using this grammar to talk about some current pollution dangers.

A Grammar in action

When Ana tries to start her car next morning to go to interview Alison, she turns the key – and nothing happens. So she looks at the **Instructions** her hire company has given her.

Then Ana phones the number she has found.

What advice do you think she gets?

➢ Problems ➢ Problems ➢ Problems ➢

Instructions

Of course we hope you will have a trouble-free time. But if you have any problems, you can call us free of charge on 0800 500900.

Please remember

➢ If you have an accident, please get the name and address of the other person involved.

➢ If you leave the car, please lock all the doors and place valuables out of sight.

Please remember also

➢ If you return the car later than the agreed time, you will have to pay extra.

➢ If you return the car in a dirty condition, you may have to pay for cleaning.

Thank you for your co-operation

B Using the grammar in your situation

Work in a group of five or six.

Here are some problem areas.
- You can't sleep at night.
- Your fifteen-year-old daughter spends all her time in front of the TV.
- You just cannot remember English vocabulary after the class.

Pick one of these problem areas (or any other similar one) and build a chain round the group.

I can't sleep at night.

If you can't sleep at night, have a glass of whisky before you go to bed.

If I have a glass of whisky before I go to bed, . . .

______________________________ .

C Using the grammar in a new situation

Work in a group of three.

What will happen or might happen?

1 If the amount of pollution in the Rhine continues to rise, ______________________________ .
2 If the ozone layer continues to be destroyed by man-made chemicals, ____________________ .
3 If global warming continues, ______________________________ .
4 If current trends continue, the destruction of tropical forests ______________________ .
5 If a pollution incident occurs in one country, ______________________________ .

What about you? What is the biggest threat you face in the immediate future in your area?

Interaction module

In this module you are going to:

- ★ listen to three short dialogues and fill in the missing words.
- ★ discuss your plans for next weekend.
- ★ ask your partners about their plans.

A Plans for the weekend

Work on your own, then with a partner.

Listen to these three conversations between different neighbours and write the missing words in the dialogues.

Compare your answers with your partner's.

1

- ● *Have you got any plans for the weekend?*
- ◆ *It __________ on the weather really. I'll probably work in the garden if it stays dry.*
- ● *The forecast doesn't sound very good for the weekend. They said gales and __________ rain are expected.*
- ◆ *Oh well, if it rains, I'll do some work in the house instead.*

2

- ● *Are you doing anything __________ this weekend?*
- ◆ *I was hoping to go __________ , but the weather forecast doesn't sound very good.*
- ● *I expect it'll be alright. The forecast is usually wrong.*
- ◆ *You can never be sure. If the weather is good when you start out, it often ________ very quickly out at sea.*

3

- ● *Are you going __________ this weekend?*
- ◆ *We were planning to take the children to the seaside.*
- ● *Haven't you heard the weather forecast? There are going to be __________ and heavy rain in all __________ on Saturday and Sunday; they said the rain may continue until midday on Monday.*
- ◆ *If the weather is bad, we shall have to find something __________ to do.*

B Different types of plans

Work with a partner.

Look at the dialogues again and find another example of where the neighbours are doing the following.

Asking about future plans
Have you got any plans for the weekend?

____

Describing plans which could be changed
We were planning to take the children to the seaside.

____

Warning someone about bad weather
The forecast doesn't sound very good for the weekend.

____

Talking about alternative plans
Oh well, if it rains, I'll do some work in the house instead.

____

C Your plans

Work on your own, then in small groups.

Make a list of things you were planning to do next weekend.
How many of these things depend on the weather?
Make a list of alternative things you can do if the weather is not suitable.

Now discuss your weekend plans with your group in the same way that the neighbours discuss their plans.

Include the following in your discussions:
- asking about future plans.
- warning someone about bad weather.
- describing plans which could be changed.
- talking about alternative plans.

Module Banks

To complete your work in this session, choose one of the modules from the Block Two Module Banks, starting on page 87. You can do these modules in any order you choose.

Summary

Grammar conditionals 1
– If the car does not start, please check that there is petrol in the tank.
– If you return the car later than the agreed time, you will have to pay extra.
– If you return the car in a dirty condition, you will have to pay extra.

Interaction
– Have you got any plans for the weekend?
– Are you doing anything interesting this weekend?
– Are you going anywhere this weekend?
– I'll probably work in the garden if it stays dry.
– I was hoping to go sailing, but the weather forecast doesn't sound very good.
– We were planning to take the children to the seaside.

Review

Work on your own at home after the session.

1 Fill in the Record Chart on page 101. Look through the Summary at the top of this page and remember the activities you did in class.

2 From the module you chose from the Module Banks, write down here:
Three key words you want to remember.

__________ __________ __________

Three key phrases or structures you want to remember.

__________ __________ __________

Grammar module conditionals

In this module you are going to:
★ look at some examples of this grammar point in action.
★ practise using this grammar to talk about changes in your life.
★ practise using this grammar to explore some ideas about the media.

A Grammar in action

On her way to catch the ferry back home, Ana gets stuck in a traffic jam on the M4. Here is what she thinks to herself.

If I had left an hour earlier, I would have had plenty of time.
If I hadn't had lunch with Alison, I could have left earlier.
If I had caught the train to the airport, I would have avoided the jam.
If I turned off the motorway, I might avoid the jam.
If I left the car in Swindon, I could catch the train from there and fly back.

B Using the grammar in your situation

Work on your own, then with a partner.

A Different Life

Think of five ways your life would have been, or might have been, different.

If I had ____________ */hadn't* ______________ *, I would / might (not) have* ________________ .

Share some of these with a partner. Do you have any in common?

C Using the grammar in a new situation

Work in a group of three.

Complete these sentences with the right words.

1 If serious Sunday newspapers (not weigh) ____________ so much, maybe more people would read them.
2 More people might go to the cinema, if it (not cost) ____________ so much.
3 If museums and art galleries (try) ____________ harder to attract young people, maybe they (can bring) ____________ in a wider audience.
4 If commercial television channels (show) ____________ fewer American programmes, European programmes might have a better chance of being shown.
5 If radio stations (play) ____________ less pop music, there (be) ____________ more time for them to broadcast advertisements, which are much more interesting.

What about you? Now change the sentences in any way you like to make them more interesting – or more true.

If serious Sunday newspapers weighed more, maybe their readers would be stronger.

Writing module

In this module you are going to practise:
- ★ completing a description from notes.
- ★ writing a description from notes.

A Interview notes

Work on your own.

When she returns to Brussels, Ana Vasquez starts work on her profile of Alison Steadman. She starts by looking at the notes she made after her interview.

EMPLOYEE PROFILE: INTERVIEW NOTES

NAME *Alison Steadman*
JOB TITLE *Sales Executive*
PERSONAL BACKGROUND *Married.*
No children (yet!)
LENGTH OF TIME WITH INTEX *5 years*
LENGTH OF TIME IN PRESENT JOB
2 years (previously sales assistant)
SPECIAL TRAINING
Diploma in Marketing
she is learning French at evening classes
AMBITION
To have the opportunity to work at one of the other centres in Europe.

B Completing a description

Work on your own, then with a partner.

Complete this description of Alison – using the notes.

Alison Steadman works in ____________ as a ____________ . She has worked for INTEX ____________ . Before she moved into her present job ____________ years ago, she worked for ____________ years as a ____________ . Alison is very well qualified for her job. She has a ____________ and is studying ____________ at evening classes. Alison is married and she may think about having children in the future. Her ambition is ____________ .

Compare your description with a partner.

C Interviewing and writing a description

Work with a partner.

Interview your partner to find out the same information that Ana has found out about Alison.

Then write a description of your partner.

10

Module Banks

To complete your work in this session, choose one of the modules from the Block Two Module Banks. You can do these modules in any order you choose.

Summary

Grammar conditionals 2

– If I had left an hour earlier, I would have had plenty of time.
– If I hadn't had lunch with Alison, I could have left earlier.
– If I turned off the motorway, I might avoid the jam.
– If newspapers did not weigh so much, maybe more people would read them.

Writing

– . . . works in . . . as a . . . . • She has worked for . . . since . . . . • Before she moved into her present job . . . years ago, she worked for . . . years as a . . . . • She has a . . . qualification and is studying . . . at evening classes. • Her ambition is . . . .

Review

Work on your own at home after the session.

1 Fill in the Record Chart on page 101. Look through the Summary at the top of this page and remember the activities you did in class.

2 From the module you chose from the Module Banks, write down here:
Three key words you want to remember.

__________ __________ __________

Three key phrases or structures you want to remember.

__________ __________ __________

Block Two 11

Listening module

In this module you are going to:

★ listen to a telephone conversation and write the missing words in a message.
★ listen to a telephone conversation and write the missing words and phrases in a message.
★ make notes on one part of a telephone conversation and practise reading the conversation with your partner.

A Missing words

Work on your own.

When Ana gets back to the office in Brussels, she finds a number of phone messages.

One of the messages is from Yves Lanson, a technical operations manager at the INTEX Fibre Manufacturing Centre in Lyon. Ana has arranged to visit Yves in Lyon and interview him for the new company brochure.

Listen to the conversation and add the missing words to the message that Antje Miedema writes for Ana Vasquez.

TELEPHONE MESSAGE

Call taken by *Antje Miedema*
For *Ana Vasquez*
Date *March*
Time *15.30*
From ____________

Meeting on . . . . and . . . .
March not possible. Emergency visit to
. . . . on business. Please
. . . . appointment. Will contact
you on . . . . morning to
re-arrange appointment.

B Missing words and phrases

Work on your own.

The second message is from Maria Cellini, an old friend of Ana's. Maria is a design consultant at COMOTEX, the INTEX joint venture hosiery manufacturing centre in Como. Ana hopes to do a profile of Maria for the new company brochure. Listen to the conversation and add the missing words and phrases to the message.

TELEPHONE MESSAGE

Call taken by *Antje Miedema*
For *Ana Vasquez*
Date *9th March*
Time *14.00*
From ______________________

.... urgent. Maria has .... a room at ....
for .... because her mother ....
You .... on 25th/26th. If .... phone
her ....

C Re-creating a conversation

Work with a partner.

Listen to one of the parts in the following telephone conversation and fill in the missing words. Your partner will do the same with the other part. When you have filled in the missing words, practise reading the conversation aloud with your partner.

Antje *Hallo, Marketing, Antje Miedema __________ .*
Alison *Hallo. __________ like to speak to Ana Vasquez, please.*
Antje *Hold __________ a moment please __________ . Hallo, I'm afraid she's just __________ to lunch.*
Alison *Could you give her a __________ , please. Tell her that Alison Steadman phoned and that she left her __________ in my office. I'll send them on to her by post.*
Antje *Shall I ask her to phone you __________ .*
Alison *No, it isn't __________ .*
Antje *I'll give her the __________ as soon as she gets __________ from lunch.*
Alison *Thanks. Goodbye.*
Antje *Goodbye.*

11

Grammar module indirect questions and commands

In this module you are going to:

★ look at some examples of this grammar point in action.

★ practise using this grammar point in your situation.

★ practise using this grammar point in relation to signs.

A Grammar in Action

Ana hopes that her new brochure for INTEX will answer a number of questions for staff and clients.

- What does the company produce?
- Where does it have factories?
- How many employees work for it?
- What sort of people are they?
- Is the company expanding?
- Are there plans to develop new products?

Here she is explaining her hopes for the brochure to her colleagues in the marketing department.

Look at the way the questions appear in what Ana says.

I hope this brochure will answer a lot of questions for our clients, and for our staff. They want to know what the company produces. Many of our staff ask where it has factories and wonder how many people work for it. And of course they wonder what sort of people they are. They also wonder if the company is expanding and ask if there are plans to develop new products.

Some of Ana's colleagues have doubts and suggestions.

Franz *I think you should have a lot more photographs.*
Franz suggested she should have a lot more photographs.

Silvia *Don't put too many details about new developments in the brochure.*
Silvia told her not to put too many details about new developments in the brochure.

Eduardo *Please don't interview staff from my department.*
Eduardo asked her not to interview staff from his department.

B Using this grammar in your situation

Work in a group of three.

Ask one partner questions about the other partner. Use *Wh*-questions and open questions. Take turns like this:

Steffi (to André)	*How many children has Georg got?*
André (to Georg)	*Steffi wonders/would like to know how many children you have got.*
Georg	*I've got three – two girls and a boy.*

C Signs

Work in a group of three.

What do these signs mean?

It asks you (not) to . . . .
It tells you (not) to . . . .
It suggests you should . . . .

Write some more signs like these in your language. Can your partners explain them to a visitor to your country?

1 PLEASE AVOID LEAVING LITTER

2 

3 POLITE NOTICE
Please do not park outside my window

4 FIRE DANGER
Please do not light fire, drop matches or cigarettes ends

5 

6 

7 ROAD CLOSED AT CAWSTON
RECOMMENDED DIVERSION
VIA HORSFORD

Module Banks

To complete your work in this session, choose one of the modules from the Block Two Module Banks. You can do these modules in any order you choose.

Summary

Listening
– My name is . . . , I'd like to speak to . . . please.
– I'm phoning about . . .
– Could you tell her . . .
– Could you give her a message please.

Learning Tip
When you are listening to people talking in your own language it is possible to understand what they are saying without understanding every word they say. The same is true when you are listening to people speaking in English. You will not be expected to understand every word in any of the listening modules in this book. If you hear an unfamiliar word, don't waste time trying to understand the meaning because you will miss the words that come after it and probably lose the sense of what the person is saying.

Grammar indirect questions and commands
– I hope this brochure will answer a lot of questions for our clients, and for our staff. They want to know what the company produces. Many of our staff ask where it has factories and wonder how many people work for it. And of course they wonder what sort of people they are. They also wonder if the company is expanding and ask if there are plans to develop new products.

– *Franz* *I think you should have a lot more photographs.*
Franz suggested she should have a lot more photographs.

– *Silvia* *Don't put too many details about new developments in the brochure.*
Silvia told her not to put too many details about new developments in the brochure.

– *Eduardo* *Please don't interview staff from my department.*
Eduardo asked her not to interview staff from his department.

Review

Work on your own at home after the session.

1 Fill in the Record Chart on page 101. Look through the Summary at the top of this page and remember the activities you did in class.

2 From the module you chose from the Module Banks, write down here:
Three key words you want to remember.

__________ __________ __________

Three key phrases or structures you want to remember.

__________ __________ __________

Grammar module past simple and past continuous; past perfect

In this module you are going to:
- ★ look at some examples of this grammar point in action.
- ★ practise using this grammar point to talk about some of the characters in English for Europe.
- ★ practise using this grammar point in your situation.

A Grammar in action

Do you remember what happened when Ana Vasquez arrived in Gloucester to talk to Alison Steadman?

Look carefully at these three sentences and at the verb tenses used.

1 When Ana Vasquez arrived at her hotel in Gloucester, she found that Alison was not there.
2 When Ana Vasquez arrived at her hotel in Gloucester, she found that Alison was taking part in a meeting in another town.
3 When Ana Vasquez arrived at her hotel in Gloucester, she found that Alison had left for a meeting in another town.
4 Ana Vasquez arrived at her hotel while Alison was taking part in a meeting in another town.
5 Ana Vasquez arrived at her hotel in Gloucester after Alison had left for a meeting in another town.

B Using this grammar in new situations

Work in groups of three.

Complete these sentences.

1 *While Ana was driving . . . .*
2 *When Ana got back to the office, she found that . . . .*
3 *After Ana had left, Alison . . . .*
4 *When Ana had completed her article about Alison, ...*
5 *When Ana phoned Yves Lanson in Lyon, he was . . . .*

C Using this grammar in your situation

Work in groups of three.

On November 9th 1989 the Berlin Wall came down.
What were you doing when you heard the news?
What had happened before the Wall came down?

Reading module

In this module you are going to:
★ match words from the text with their definitions.
★ make notes about the two main people in a news story.
★ complete sentences using information from the text.

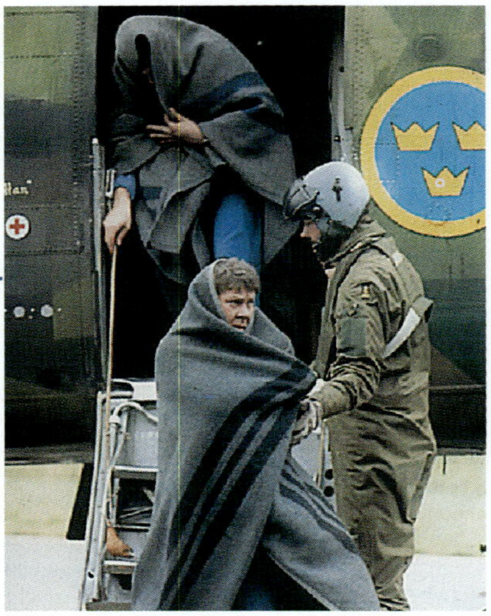

A Matching words and definitions

Work on your own and with a partner.

On 28th September, 1994, the car ferry, **Estonia**, sank as it was travelling from Estonia to Sweden. Over nine hundred people died.

Before you read the newspaper article, match the following five definitions with words which are used in the article:

1 a sign or sound that tells other people that someone is in danger and needs help.
2 a small, flat boat carried on a ship or plane. Passengers use it to escape when there is an emergency.
3 a plastic or rubber sleeveless jacket that can be filled with air. People wear one to keep them afloat in water.
4 an event that causes a lot of deaths and damage.
5 someone who continues to live after a dangerous situation where other people have died – sometimes used to describe a thing as well as a person.

life raft ❑ life jacket ❑ survivor ❑ distress signal ❑ disaster ❑

Check your answers with your partner.

B Making notes

Work on your own and with a partner.

Skim read the newspaper article, then read it again and write the missing information about the two main people in the story in the table.

	Person 1	Person 2
Family Name	Oun	
First Name		Jannu
Age		
Profession		
Married/Single		Single
Number of children		None
Reason for travelling on the Estonia		

Using his camera flash to attract ships, one ferry passenger captured the drama on film. But who was the man in the lifejacket?

Photos reunite Estonia survivors

Julie Read reports on a remarkable friendship which sprang from tragedy

The last time 34-year-old Swedish engineer Mikael Oun saw Jannu Aser, the 21-year-old Tallinn computer technician was swathed in lifejackets and clinging despairingly to the steeply pitched deck of the doomed ferry *Estonia*.

When Oun met Aser again on 10 November, it was the most unlikely reunion imaginable, a rare heart-warming moment to come out of a tragedy in which some 900 people lost their lives. Each man, after all, had believed the other to have perished in the disaster.

Remarkably, the two survivors were brought together by a photograph which Oun did not even know he had taken.

The picture was taken seconds before Oun was swept from the *Estonia's* deck into the sea. "I was using the camera's flash gun to send distress signals to other ships rather than to take pictures. I did not even look through the viewfinder," he said.

Only when he returned to his wife and three small children in Stockholm did Oun discover that the photographs he had taken had survived. Among them were two sills of an unknown man swathed in lifejackets. The pictures were published in seven Swedish newspapers, and all asked the same question: "What was this man's fate?"

Meanwhile, across the Baltic Sea, Aser was back at work listening to a local radio programme on which the pictures were being discussed. The story struck a chord. Aser went out to buy the Finnish paper *Iltal Sanomat* which had also picked up the story.

"It was only then that I realised the the unknown man was me," Aser said.

The disaster had struck during Aser's first trip to Sweden to attend a computer exhibition.

Aser jumped off the ship when the waves became too great and landed on a lifraft. He was eventually picked up by a helicopter and taken to a Finnish ferry. Neither his boss nor his boss's son survived the ordeal.

Oun had travelled to Tallinn on board the *Estonia* as a volunteer driver for a Stockholm-based charity to distribute aid to Estonians.

It was when the boat suddenly heeled over violently and all his luggage fell against the door that Oun knew he had to get out.

He picked up his camera, which had fal out of a bag, and wedged open the door. Once outside the cabin Oun found the stairs. Standing at 1.9 metres tall, he was able to pull himself up by grabbing on to handrails that were beyond other people's reach.

"I don't know if it was shock or panic or just the survival instinct, but I felt no pain and do not remember hearing anything," he told *The European*. "There were wounds on my feet afterwards but I was quite numb at the time. If I had known then that the bottom of the ship was full of water, I don't think I would have remained quite so calm."

When he had hauled himself from the interior of the ship, he made his way to the bow, and that is where he came across Aser. Looking down, he noticed that the bridge was completely under water. "I knew then that the ship was doomed," he said.

"I decided to use the camera's flash gun to tray to send out distress signals to other ships whose lights I could see in the distance. I put the camera back in my pocket and then seconds later a huge wave crashed on to the deck, stripped me of my lifejacket and swept me into the sea."

"I emerged on the surface of the water to find myself between two life-rafts. I clambered into one and, with the eight others on board, pulled another three on board. We huddled together to keep warm."

When Oun and Aser met again, they spent an emotional three hours in comparing their experiences, with the aid of an interpreter.

"I was overjoyed that Jannu had survived as well," said Oun. ■

C Using information from the text

Work on your own and with a partner.

Some words are missing from each of the sentences below.
Read the sentences, then re-read the text in order to find the missing information.
Complete each of the sentences with the missing information.

1 After Mikael ______________ the photograph of Jannu, a wave swept him into the sea.
2 After Jannu had jumped off the ship, he ________ on a life raft and ________________ by a helicopter.

3 Each man thought that the other ____________ .
4 Mikael did not know that he ____________ a picture of Jannu.
5 The newspapers ________ to know what __________________ to the man in the pictures.
6 Jannu _________ about the photographs of the unknown man while he _________________ to a local radio programme.
7 Jannu realised that he ________ the unknown man when he ________ the photographs in a Finnish newspaper.
8 When Mikael and Jannu ________ again they ________ , with the help of interpreters, about what ____________ to them on that terrible night in September.

Module Banks

To complete your work in this session, choose one of the modules from the Block Two Module Banks. You can do these modules in any order you choose.

Summary

Grammar past simple and past continuous; past perfect

– When Ana Vasquez arrived at her hotel in Gloucester, she found that Alison was not there.
– When Ana Vasquez arrived at her hotel in Gloucester, she found that Alison was taking part in a meeting in another town.
– When Ana Vasquez arrived at her hotel in Gloucester, she found that Alison had left for a meeting in another town.
– Ana Vasquez arrived at her hotel while Alison was taking part in a meeting in another town.
– Ana Vasquez arrived at her hotel in Gloucester after Alison had left for a meeting in another town.

Reading

– What were the words from the text you matched with their definitions?
– Who were the two people in the story?
– Can you remember the sentences you completed about them?

Review

Work on your own at home after the session.

1 Fill in the Record Chart on page 101. Look through the Summary at the top of this page and remember the activities you did in class.

2 From the module you chose from the Module Banks, write down here:
Three key words you want to remember.

______________________ ______________________ ______________________

Three key phrases or structures you want to remember.

______________________ ______________________ ______________________

Grammar module quantifiers: countables and uncountables

In this module you are going to:

- ★ look at some examples of this grammar point in action.
- ★ practise using this grammar point to talk about some European towns.
- ★ practise using this grammar point in your situation.

A Grammar in action

Look at these sentences. Think of a town or city in Europe that each sentence could describe.

There is usually quite a lot of snow in winter.
There are a lot of days when the temperature is over 25°.
There are a few days when it is foggy, but not as many as people expect.
There are very few days when you don't see the sun.
There isn't much snow most years, but sometimes there is a lot.
There aren't many days in a year when you can go sunbathing.

Look carefully at the sentences.
See how different quantifiers (*a lot of/much/many/a few*) are used with plurals (*days*) and uncountables (*snow*).

B Using this grammar in new situations

Work on your own, then in a group of three.

Here are some comments made by people who live in different European cities. Complete what they say.

1 London used to be a very attractive city, but now there is a ________ of traffic – too much, I think.
2 I love living in Barcelona. There are so ________ things to do and such an exciting atmosphere.
3 Cologne is a very modern city, but there are still a ________ old buildings in the city centre.
4 There are not ________ European cities which are as beautiful as Bruges.
5 The nice thing about living in Amsterdam is that there are a ________ of open spaces and green areas.
6 Cork is only a small place, but there isn't ________ pollution and everybody is very friendly.

C Using this grammar in your situation

Work in a group of three.

Use the quantifiers you have practised to make sentences about your town or region.

Interaction module

In this module you are going to:

- ★ listen to some conversations at a dinner party and add the missing words to the text of some of the conversations.
- ★ role-play a dinner party with the other members of your group.

A Conversations

Work on your own and with a partner.

Some of Ana Vazquez's colleagues from INTEX centres in other countries have come to Brussels for a conference. Ana and her husband, Ralf Staelens, have invited them to dinner at their house on the outskirts of Brussels.

Listen to the recordings and fill in the missing words in the conversations.

Welcoming

Ana	*I'll go. I expect that's Pablo. Could you get everyone a drink, Ralf?*
Ralf	*OK.*
Ana	*Ah, Pablo. I'm ____________ you could ____________ it.*
Pablo	*Hello Ana. Sorry I'm a bit late; I got stuck in the traffic. These are for you.*
Ana	*That's very kind of you. They're beautiful . . . I love roses. ____________ me ____________ your coat. The others are in here.*
Ralf	*I'll get it.*
Lorenza	*Good evening. My name is Lorenza Masari.*
Ralf	*Please ____________ in. ____________ I take your coat?*
Lorenza	*Thank you.*

Arranging the seating

Ana	*Right everybody. I think we are ready to eat now. ____________ you like to come ____________ to the dining room?*
All	*Oh . . . right . . . certainly . . .*
Bruce	*Where would you like us to sit?*
Ana	*Would you ____________ to sit here, Bruce, next to me and ____________ Lorenza could sit next to you. Martina do you ____________ sitting by Ralf and Pablo here by me. Yves, I've ____________ you next to Martina and Alison next to Pablo.*

Offering/accepting/declining

Alison	*Could you ____________ the salad, please?*
Pablo	*Certainly. Here you are. Can I pass you anything?*
Ana	*No, thank you.*
Lorenza	*Would you like some ____________ cheese?*
Bruce	*No thank you, I couldn't eat ____________ thing.*
Lorenza	*What about you Ralf?*
Ralf	*No, thank you. I've ____________ got some.*
Ana	*____________ coffee?*
Bruce	*Yes, please.*
Ana	*Milk?*
Bruce	*Yes, please.*
Ana	*How ____________ ?*
Bruce	*Just a ____________ please.*
Ana	*Say ____________ .*
Bruce	*That's fine.Thank you.*

Saying goodbye

Bruce	*Thank you for a ____________ meal.*
	See you tomorrow.
Ana	*Thank you for coming. Goodbye.*
Pablo	*It was ____________ Ana. Thanks.*
Ana	*I'm glad you were able to come. Bye.*
Alison	*Thank you for a very nice evening, Ana.*
Ana	*It was a ____________ . See you in the morning.*
Martina	*Goodbye and thank you. It was a wonderful evening.*
Ana	*I'm ____________ you could come. Goodbye*
Yves	*Thanks very much. I really enjoyed myself.*
Ana	*Good. See you tomorrow.*
Lorenza	*It was a lovely evening. Thank you.*
Ana	*It was ____________ nice to see you again. Bye.*

Check your answers with your partner.

B A dinner party

Work in a group of six.

Imagine that the people in your group are the guests at a dinner party at your home. One of you is the host or hostess.

The host/hostess:

- welcomes the guests.
- introduces the guests to one another.
- tells the guests where he/ she would like them to sit.

When you are all sitting at the table, each person should:

- offer someone something.
- ask someone for something.
- accept something that is offered.
- decline something that is offered.

Each person in the group says goodbye at the end of the evening.

Module Banks

To complete your work in this session, choose one of the modules from the Block Two Module Banks. You can do these modules in any order you choose.

Summary

Grammar quantifiers: countables and uncountables
- There is usually quite a lot of snow in winter.
- There are a lot of days when the temperature is over 25°.
- There are a few days when it is foggy, but not as many as people expect.
- There are very few days when you don't see the sun.
- There isn't much snow most years, but sometimes there is a lot.
- There aren't many days in a year when you can go sunbathing.

Interaction
- Can you remember some of the language used for: welcoming? • arranging the seating? • offering? • accepting? • declining?

Review

Work on your own at home after the session.

1 Fill in the Record Chart on page 101. Look through the Summary at the top of this page and remember the activities you did in class.

2 From the module you chose from the Module Banks, write down here:
Three key words you want to remember.

__________ __________ __________

Three key phrases or structures you want to remember.

__________ __________ __________

Grammar module present perfect and past perfect: simple and continuous

In this module you are going to:
- ★ look at some examples of this grammar point in action.
- ★ practise using this grammar point to build up profiles of two people.
- ★ practise using this grammar point in your situation.

A Grammar in action

Here is a profile of Martina Dege who works for INTEX at their research centre in Magdeburg.

Look carefully at the tenses in each sentence, *Martina Dege:*

- has lived in Magdeburg all her life.
- has been working for INTEX for four years.
- had studied chemical engineering at university for five years before she joined the company.
- had been working for INTEX for two years when she got married.
- has visited the company's plants in France and Italy.
- has never been to England but hopes to go there on holiday soon.

B Building new profiles

Work in groups of three.

Build up profiles of these two people who also work for INTEX. Use the sentences given and add some more of your own.

Françoise Duclerc:

____
____
____
____
____

Paolo Rezzi:

____
____
____
____
____

- has been working for INTEX for fifteen years.
- has been living in Lyon for two years.
- had worked for INTEX in Brussels before she moved to Lyon.
- has lived in the Como region all his life.
- had worked for another textile firm before he joined INTEX.

C Using this grammar in your situation

Work in a group of three.

Think of a person likely to be known to the other people in your class (e. g. a politician, a sports person – or somebody local).

Make up five sentences about this person like the ones you have practised about the INTEX employees.

Read the sentences out one at a time. How quickly can the class guess who you are describing?

Writing module

In this module you are going to:

★ draft and re-draft a formal letter.

You would like to take out a subscription to The European.

A Planning

Work on your own, then in groups of three.

- How will you give your address?
- Will you include the address of The European.
- How will you start the letter?
- How will you end the letter?

B Drafting

Write to the address given. Tell them:

- when you want the subscription to start.
- the address to send the copies to.
- how you would like to pay.

C Re-drafting

Look at what your colleagues have written and re-draft your letter to include any changes you want to make.

ENJOY AN INTERNATIONAL OUTLOOK

(AT LOCAL PRICES)

Start a subscription to The European and receive regular coverage of European events. Improved payment options allow you to pay in the manne that is most convenient for you – cheque, credit card, giro or bank transfer – ALL IN YOUR LOCAL CURRENCY.
See why The European is the only newspaper for Europe

Europe Price per country*		6 months (26 issues)	12 months (52 issues)
Austria	Ausst Sch	775	1,384
Belgium	F	1,300	2,400
Czech Republic	K˘cs	1,800	3,400
Denmark	Kr	395	710
Finland	Markka	328	590
France	Ffr	310	570
Germany	Dm	95	175
Greece	Dr	10,000	19,000
Ireland (Rep.)	IR£	29	52
Italy	Lira	72,800	137,000
Netherlands	Nfl	100	185
Norway	Kr	430	780
Portugal	Esc	10,000	17,800
Russia	£	40	80
Spain	Pts	7,600	13,500
Sweden	Kr	489	880
Switzerland	Sfr	85	150
Turkey	Tl	1,520,000	2,700,000
Other Europe	£	40	80

* All local currency cheques must be drawn on a local bank. To pay by local giro or bank transfer tick *'Please invoice me'* and the term you prefer. Bank details will be forwarded to you. Please allow 3 weeks for order processing.

Please fax or send your subscription form to:
Europe & All other: The European, PO Box 14, Harold Hill, Romford RM3 8EQ, UK. Tel: + 44 (0) 708 340143 Fax: + 44 (0) 708 340132
USA & Canada: The European, PO Box 3000, Denville, NJ 07834 USA. Tel: + 1 (201)627 2997 or (800) 875 2997 (US only) Fax: + 1 (201) 627 5872
Japan: Barclay Vouchers Co Ltd, 7th floor, Sanbancho MS Bldg, 20, Sanban-cho, Chiyoda-Ku, Tokyo 102, Japan. Tel: +81 3 3234 5311 Fax: +81 3 3234 7031
Singapore/Malaysia: JAC Recruitment, 138 Robinson Rd, 14-10, Hong Leong Centre, Singapore 0106 Tel: + 65 224 6864 Fax: + 65 224 9473
Czech Republic & Russia: PPI – Rinance and Data Services, PO Box 8004, 2130 PA Hoofdorp, The Netherlands. Tel: + 31 2503 87204 Fax: + 31 2503 53832

THE EUROPEAN
THE WEEKLY NEWSPAPER FOR EUROPE

DELIVERED TO YOUR DOO

Module Banks

To complete your work in this session, choose one of the modules from the Block Two Module Banks. You can do these modules in any order you choose.

Summary

Grammar present perfect and past perfect: simple and continuous

Martina Dege:
- has lived in Magdeburg all her life.
- has been working for INTEX for four years.
- had studied chemical engineering at university for five years before she joined the company.
- had been working for INTEX for two years when she got married.
- has visited the company's plants in France and Italy.
- has never been to England but hopes to go there on holiday soon.

Writing
- How did you give your address?
- Did you include the address of **The European**?
- How did you start the letter?
- How did you end the letter?

Review

Work on your own at home after the session.

1 Fill in the Record Chart on page 101. Look through the Summary at the top of this page and remember the activities you did in class.

2 From the module you chose from the Module Banks, write down here:
Three key words you want to remember.

__________ __________ __________

Three key phrases or structures you want to remember.

__________ __________ __________

Reading module

In this module you are going to:

★ scan a newspaper article for specific information in order to deduce the title of a diagram.
★ give your opinion about some characteristics of other countries.
★ compare your opinions with the results of an opinion survey.

A What are these charts about?

Work on your own and with a partner.

Read the newspaper article about a survey of how Europeans see people in other countries.
Some of the results of this opinion survey appear in the text.
Use the information in the text to help you match the four headings with the four charts showing the results of the opinion survey.

Check your answers with a partner.

A country where I would like to retire

The inhabitants are friendly and cheerful

People here keep their promises

A country where I would like to work

Feel good in Spain and Italy and feel sorry

Rory Watson
Brussels

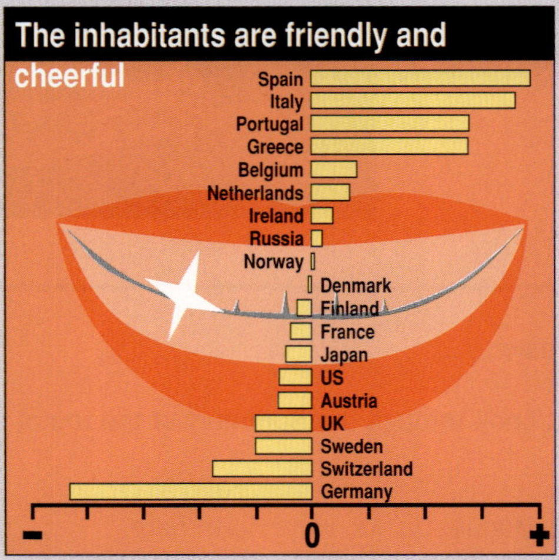

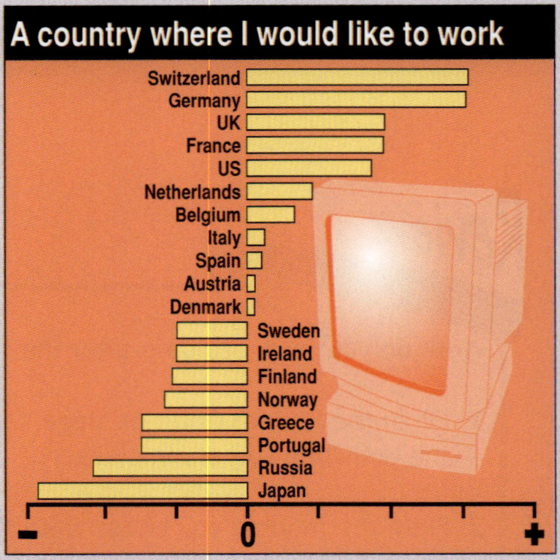

RESEARCHERS are closer to understanding the mysterious "feel-good factor" that makes some countries and nationalities appear more attractive than others.
A survey of the way Europeans view each other, and countries further afield, has dispelled some myths but, sadly, confirmed more stereotypes.
One thousand people in each of 16 countries were asked to rank the three countries which, they believed, corresponded – best and worst – to a list of attributes from friendliness to good food, or in which they would choose to live, work or retire. The results were pulled together to provide a rough index of Europe's favourite places and some suggestions as to exactly why people think in the way that they do.

The poll seems to be bad news for the Swiss and Germans, who emerge as the least friendly and least cheerful of us all. But that doesn't seem to matter to the career-minded: given the chance, more people would like to work in those countries than anywhere else.
The most cheerful Europeans were the Spanish, Portuguese,

B The best and the worst

Work on your own. These were the countries included in the opinion survey.

Austria • Belgium • Denmark • Finland • France • Germany • Greece • Ireland • Italy • Japan • The Netherlands • Norway • Portugal • Russia • Spain • Sweden • Switzerland • The United Kingdom • The United States of America

Choose three countries as your answer to each question and write them in the columns **Your opinions** in the table below.

1 In which of these countries do people have good taste in food and drink?
2 Which of these countries would you not want to go to for a holiday?
3 Which of these countries preserve the environment best?
4 Which of these countries will benefit most from European integration?
5 Which of these countries do you like most?
6 Which of these countries do like like least?

Your opinions

❶		❷		❸	
1	________	1	________	1	________
2	________	2	________	2	________
3	________	3	________	3	________
4	________	4	________	4	________
5	________	5	________	5	________
6	________	6	________	6	________

for the Germans and the Swiss

People here keep their promises

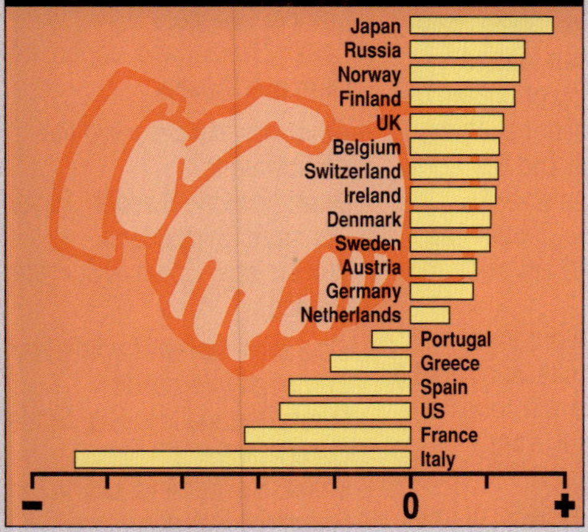

A country where I would like to retire

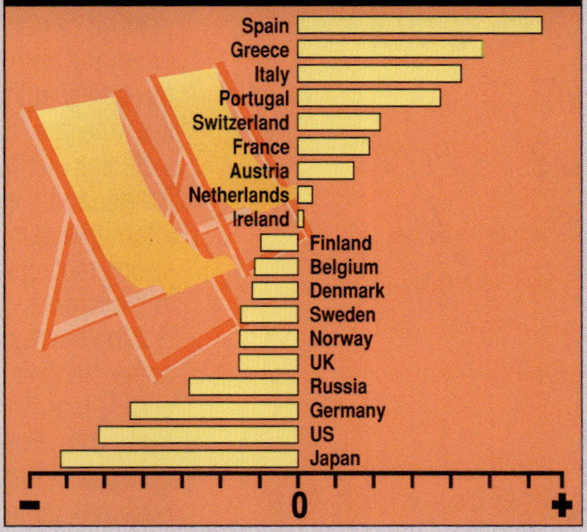

Greeks and Italians. They are also living in the countries most people want to retire to. The Italians were, however, also thought the least likely to keep their word, in contrast to the apparently more honest – the Japanese and Russians. The Norwegians, Finns, the British and Belgians are not considered the most fun-loving folk, but when they give their word they are generally believed to keep it.

The picture painted by the survey is of a Europe with a north-south divide.

If it's fun you want then head for the Mediterranean. The food is delicious, the sun shines and the people among the most attractive of all, the survey suggests.

If it is quality of life, the environment and honesty you are seeking, then Scandinavia and Switzerland might be more of a draw.

Stereotypes are an enduring trait of the European Union. For some, this confirms the folly of trying to create a closer Union. For others it is proof that EU-wide legislation is no threat to national quirks and traditions.

Country Image II is published by INRA (International Research Associates) Europe, 18 Avenue Roger Vandendriessche, 1150 Brussels Telephone: + 32/2.772.4444.

C Comparing your opinions with the results of an opinion survey

Read this article based upon an opinion survey. Compare the results of the survey with your opinions.

Compare your answers with your partner's.

The best and worst of Europe

RANKING the best and worst of sixteen countries is at best a rough guide. Large countries, with strong image, are bound to give a stronger impression, whether positive or negative. Spain, Italy, Germany and Japan feature frequently at the top or bottom of the rankings. Smaller countries, including Denmark and the Netherlands, with a weaker international image, arouse few strong feelings and are clustered in the middle.
But the survey still produced some startling results, such as the finding that Russia will benefit most, after Portugal, from European integration.
Here are some examples of the best and the worst:

Countries that have preserved real quality of life.
Best: Norway, Switzerland, Finland, Sweden, Austria.
Worst: US, Germany, Italy, Russia, Spain.

People here have good taste in food and drink.
Best: Italy, France, Spain, Greece, Portugal.
Worst: US, Britain, Japan, Sweden, Norway.

Places where people want to go on holiday.
Best: Greece, Spain, Italy, Portugal, Austria.
Worst: Germany, Belgium, Japan, Sweden, Denmark.

Men here are the most/least attractive.
Most: Italy, Spain, Greece, France, Sweden.
Least: Japan, Switzerland, Germany, Austria, Belgium.

Women here are the most/least attractive.
Most: Italy, Spain, Sweden, France, Greece.
Least: Switzerland, Japan, US, Germany, Austria.

Countries that preserve the environment.
Best: Norway, Sweden, Finland, Denmark, Switzerland.
Worst: Italy, Spain, US, France, Greece.

Countries that will benefit from European integration.
Most: Portugal, Russia, Spain, Greece, Ireland.
Least: Switzerland, US, Japan, Germany, Sweden.

Countries people like.
Most: Spain, Italy, Greece, Portugal, France.
Least: Japan, Germany, US, Belgium, Russia.

Grammar module
causatives: getting things done

In this module you are going to:
- ★ look at some examples of this grammar point in action.
- ★ practise using this grammar point in your situation.
- ★ practise using this grammar point.

A Grammar in action

Ana Vasquez is planning another trip to Gloucester to follow-up her meeting with Alison. Before she leaves, she makes a list of things to do.

black trousers cleaned
watch repaired DONE
hair trimmed??
passport renewed CHECK
money changed? NO

Look carefully at these sentences which Ana could use to say what is on her list. See how the sentences are formed.

Before I leave, I must get/have my black trousers cleaned.

It's a good job I got/had my watch repaired last week. I will need it when I'm away.

Shall I get/have my hair trimmed before I go? I'm not sure.

I think I need to get/have my passport renewed. I must check. I don't want any problems!

I don't need to get/have any money changed. I've still got about £150 in English money.

B Using this grammar point in new situations

Work in pairs or groups of three.

Last week you had your car serviced. What exactly did you get done? Add a sentence to explain why – like Ana's examples in **A**.

oil → change ✓
spark-plugs → replace ✓
new exhaust → fit ✓
flat tyre → repair ✓
headlamps → adjust ✓

C Using this grammar in your situation

Work on your own, then in groups of three.

- What about you?
- What have you had done recently, maybe in your home, or with your car?
- What are you planning to get done?

Find out about your partners.

Module Banks

To complete your work in this session, choose one of the modules from the Block Two Module Banks. You can do these modules in any order you choose.

Summary

Reading
- In which country are the inhabitants most friendly and cheerful?
- Which country would you like to retire to?
- In which country do people keep their promises?
- Which country would you most like to work in?
- Were you surprised at any of the results?

Grammar causatives: getting things done
- Before I leave, I must get/have my black trousers cleaned.
- It's a good job I got/had my watch repaired last week. I will need it when I'm away.
- Shall I get/have my hair trimmed before I go? I'm not sure.
- I think I need to get/have my passport renewed. I must check. I don't want any problems!
- I don't need to get/have any money changed . I've still got about £150 in English money.

Review

Work on your own at home after the session.

1 Fill in the Record Chart on page 101. Look through the Summary at the top of this page and remember the activities you did in class.

2 From the module you chose from the Module Banks, write down here:
Three key words you want to remember.

__________ __________ __________

Three key phrases or structures you want to remember.

__________ __________ __________

Grammar module prepositions used with adjectives, nouns and verbs

In this module you are going to:
- ★ look at some examples of this grammar point in action.
- ★ practise using this grammar point to talk about your own experiences.
- ★ practise using this grammar point to ask for tips and advice.

A Grammar in action

Alison Steadman has been on a trip to the INTEX centre in Magdeburg. It was the first time she had been to Germany. Now she is telling a friend in Gloucester about her experiences.

Look at what she says.

I was surprised at the size of the factory. And I was amazed at how cold the weather was. I was a bit disappointed to find they nearly all spoke English.
Before I went I was excited about the trip. But I was unhappy about how long I would be away from home.
And I was worried about finding my way in a strange city.
I was proud of myself because I didn't get lost at all.
I was proud of how much I said in German. And I was really proud of understanding some of what they said in German.
It was a really interesting way of finding out about their work.
I'm looking forward to going again.

B Talking about your own experiences

Work with a partner.

Think of a trip you have made. Use some of the language that Alison uses to tell your partner about it.

C Household tips and advice.

Work in groups of four.

- What is the best way of keeping flowers alive in the house?
- What is the best way of taking the cork from a bottle of wine if you haven't got a corkscrew?
- What is the best way of . . . ?

Have you got any questions like this? Who in your group can help you?

Listening module

In this module you are going to:
- ★ listen to the correct version of the weather forecast for Western Europe.
- ★ identify and correct the mistakes in the written version of the weather forecast.
- ★ make notes about the weather in different European cities.

A What has changed?

Work on your own.

You are going to hear part of the European weather forecast for the 4th to 9th February.
The text below is not the final version that was broadcast on the radio on 3rd February; some words have been corrected.
Listen to the cassette and mark the words that have been changed in the draft text.

DRAFT 2 – ***European weather forecast***

Thursday will see Atlantic weather fronts making erratic progress eastwards into northern Europe with further fronts continuing to affect north-western Europe and Scandinavia.
As a result, outbreaks of snow are expected in France, Spain, Britain, the Low Countries and Denmark. Eastern Poland, Norway and Sweden will be much warmer with occasional rain. The driest, warmest and sunniest weather is expected in central and western parts of the Mediterranean.
On Friday, sunny intervals and showers will be taking hold over Spain and Italy, western France and Britain, while the band of rain becomes slow-moving over eastern France and Germany. Further snow or sleet will fall over eastern parts of Poland, Hungary and Romania. Scandanavia will continue to see a little rain at times and the western Mediterranean will become more settled.

B The final version

Listen to the recording again and write in the correct words at the end of the line.
Compare your answers with your partner, then check them with the whole group.

C European cities

Work in groups of three.

You are going to hear a summary of weather conditions in six European cities for the next three days. Choose two cities each and fill in the table below with the missing information.

	Friday			Saturday			Sunday			Monday		
	min	max	sky	min	max	sky	min	max	sky	min	max	sky
Paris	8	11	__	__	9	CL	6	8	CL	__	9	__
Prague	__	7	CL	-2	__	__	-3	__	PC	0	6	CL
Rome	5	__	__	7	16	CL	8	15	__	5	__	RS
Stockholm	-8	-4	SS	__	0	CL	__	3	SS	__	3	__
Vienna	__	7	CL	0	__	__	0	__	PC	0	5	CL
Warsaw	-2	4	__	-1	4	CL	__	5	CL	__	__	PC

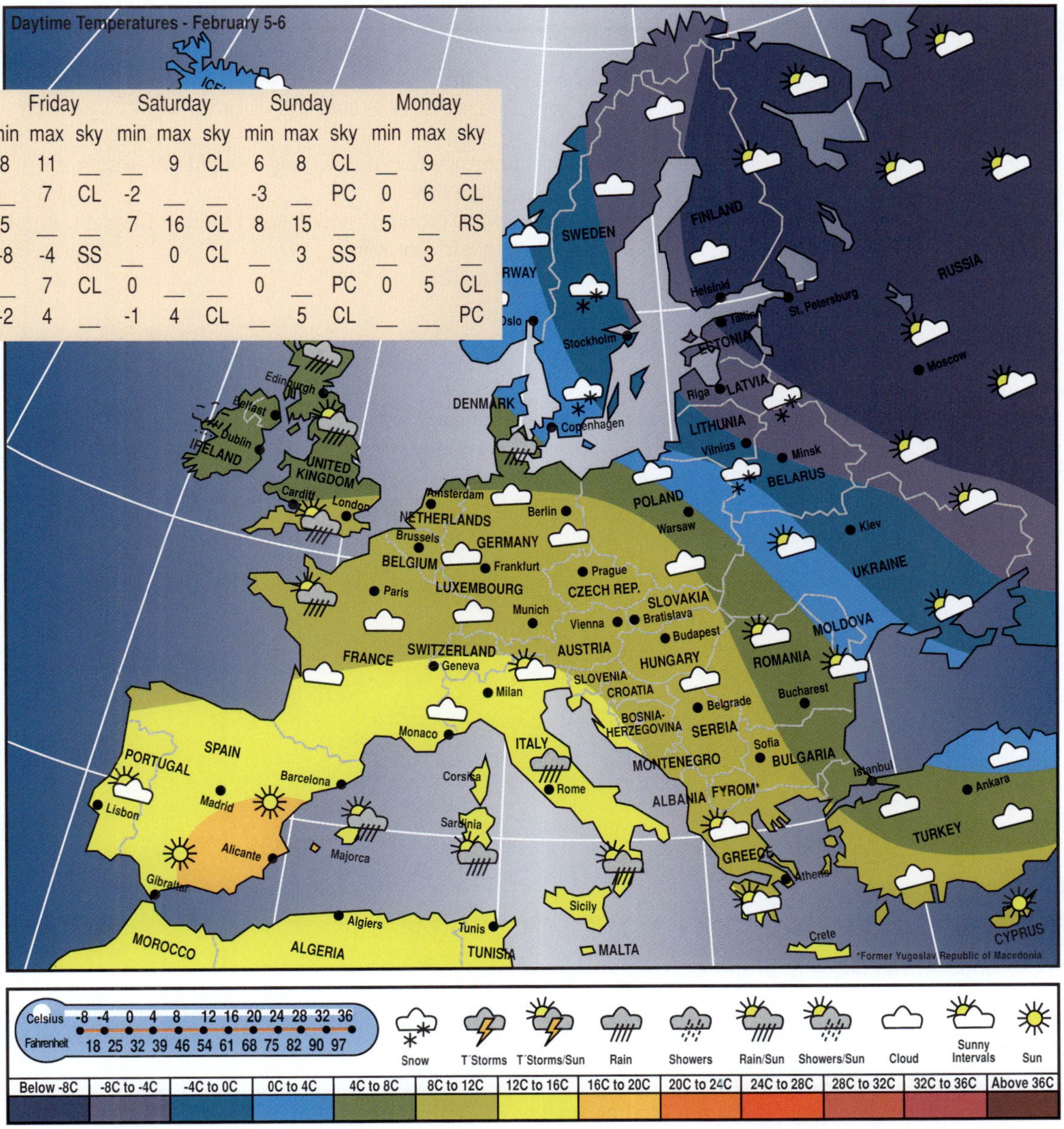

Ask your two partners to help you complete the table in order to answer the following questions.

1 Which city will have the lowest minimum temperature on Friday?
2 Which city will have snow showers on Sunday?
3 Which city will have the highest maximum temperature between Friday and Monday?
4 Which cities will have no sub-zero temperatures during this period?

Module Banks

To complete your work in this session, choose one of the modules from the Block Two Module Banks. You can do these modules in any order you choose.

Summary

Grammar prepositions used with adjectives, nouns and verbs
- I was surprised at the size of the factory. And I was amazed at how cold the weather was. I was a bit disappointed to find they nearly all spoke English.
- Before I went I was excited about the trip. But I was unhappy about how long I would be away from home. And I was worried about finding my way in a strange city.
- I was proud of myself because I didn't get lost at all. I was proud of how much I said in German. And I was really proud of understanding some of what they said in German.
- It was a really interesting way of finding out about their work.
- I'm looking forward to going again.

Listening
- Weather forecasts: What will the weather be like on Thursday? • And on Friday? • Which city will have the lowest minimum temperature on Friday? • Which city will have snow showers on Sunday?

Review

Work on your own at home after the session.

1 Fill in the Record Chart on page 101. Look through the Summary at the top of this page and remember the activities you did in class.

2 From the module you chose from the Module Banks, write down here:
Three key words you want to remember.

__________ __________ __________

Three key phrases or structures you want to remember.

__________ __________ __________

Block Two Module Banks

These are the Module Banks for Block Two.
In each session you do in class, you can choose one module from the banks to complete your work.
You can do the modules from the banks in any order.

Reading module

In this module you are going to:

- ★ match headlines with a sentence from the following article.
- ★ match headlines with newspaper articles.
- ★ give your personal reactions to newspaper articles.

A Headlines and introductions

Newspaper headlines use English verb tenses in an unusual way. Match the headlines below with the first sentence of the article that follows them.
What is the difference between the way the verb tenses are used?

U.S. President to visit Europe

Teenagers rob bank

Humber bridge re-opened after storm

Smoking banned on Underground

Rembrandt sold for record price in New York

Pope meets E.U. leaders

Electricity prices to rise next year

1 The bridge over the River Humber has been re-opened after it was closed yesterday because of dangerously high winds.
2 The President of the United States of America is going to visit Europe.
3 The Pope met leaders of countries in the European Union at a conference in Rome yesterday.
4 The cost of electricity is going to rise next year.
5 A self-portrait by the seventeenth century Dutch painter, Rembrandt van Rijn has been sold at Sotheby's in New York for a world record price.
6 Smoking has been banned on the London Underground.
7 A bank in Gloucester was robbed yesterday by a gang of four teenagers carrying toy guns.

B Headlines and newspaper articles

Work on your own and with a partner

Match the following headlines with their articles.
Write the number of the article next to the correct headline.

Youths on murder charge	❑	**Ecus find a marketplace**	❑
Venice pleads for funds	❑	**Mafia marriage blessed**	❑
Planes to help make rain	❑	**Pope's book goes on sale**	❑
Fire-raising gang arrested	❑		

C Reacting

Work in small groups.

- How do you react to those articles?
- Which is the most interesting? The most surprising? The most worrying?

Share your reactions with your colleagues.

News Briefing

1 VATICAN CITY: The first book ever published by a living pope went on sale on 19 October, with church leaders predicting it would be a best-seller. *Crossing the Threshold of Hope,* Pope John Paul II's reflections on the papacy and Catholicism, was released in 20 languages in 36 countries. All royalties from the book will go to charity, the Vatican said. Doctors have forced the Pope to cancel a visit to the United States, insisting that he needs more time to recuperate from recent hip operation.

2 ST PETERSBURG: Police arrested 22 members of a gang accused of burning alive nine local businessmen in a violent two-year spree. The criminals, who allegedly donned stolen police uniforms to carry out robberies and kidnappings, were captured in a flat on the edge of the city. Police also found three Kalashnikov rifles, seven pistols and a cache of false documents. The old tsarist capital has a reputation as a hotbed of organised crime. Earlier this year, police stopped a Lada towing a Mercedes through the city and uncovered seven bodies stuffed in the back.

3 COPENHAGEN: Three Norwegian teenagers, charged with murdering a fellow Norwegian on a ferry and dumping his body in the sea, were extradited from Denmark to Norway on 14 December. One of the men said they had stabbed the 40-year-old Norwegian as he slept in the cabin they shared on 13 December. Police said the three, aged 16, 17 and 18, allegedly stole the man's wallet containing Nkr 3,500 ($770). Crew members had detained two of the youths because they "acted suspiciously", carrying around a huge bag containing the bloodstained bedclothes.

4 TOULOUSE: The town of Blagnac, north of Toulouse, is introducing ecu coins to its local market."It is important that people feel they can touch and handle an ecu. Until now, it has merely been something that existed on paper or in the minds of politicans, financiers and Eurocrats," said Reiner Beckmann, a local businessman and coin collector who is behind the project. Local banks have produced 32,000 gold, silver and copper ecus and the banks will offer face value for the coins until 5 January when they will become collectors' items.

5 PALERMO: Eight of the nine judges investigating the mafia godfather, Toto Riina, have finally given their seal of approval to his marriage. Riina wed Antonietta Bagarella in clandestine ceremony at a church on the outskirts of Palermo in 1964. The mafia boss's home town of Corleone had long refused to recognise the ceremony legally because Riina was on the run. It had denied his residency there in an effort to rid the city of its reputation as the capital of the Cosa Nostra. Riina was on the run for nearly 24 years before being sentenced to life imprisonment last year.

6 SOFIA: Bulgaria is so short of water it may enlist the help of airplanes to try to make it rain. There is water rationing in the capital and supplies in much of the country are down to critical levels. A spokesman for the Fight Against Hail Directorate (FHD), a quasi-official body, said: "Our plan is to stimulate rain using planes." The FHD plan has been submitted to deputy prime minister Nikola Vassilev fo approval. Using a technique known as seeding, the planes would scatter particles into clouds to encourage raindrops to form.

7 VENICE: Massimo Cacciare, mayor of Venice, appealed to the Italian government on 30 November for extra funds to save the crumbling and sinking city. Cacciare said restoration projects would have to be halted and no new work could be ordered without more money. The appeal comes at a critical time for the government of Prime Minister Silvio Berluscone, whose 1995 austerity budget faces a tough battle in the Senate. City officials say Venice has sunk 23 cm in the past century.

Writing module

In this module you are going to:
- ★ find specific information in newspaper advertisements.
- ★ write a short text advertising your skills.
- ★ check and correct an advertisement.

A Finding specific information

Work on your own and with a partner.

THE EUROPEAN

EUROPEAN NEWSPAPER OF THE YEAR – page 26

22. December 1994

Advertise your skills free of charge

❶ **YOUNG** Italian woman, 28, seeks career in hotel management and/or tourism industry. Diploma in tourism industry. Worked in UK and France, fluent Italien, English and French, knowledge of German. Previous employment hotel receptionist, secretary and sales and marketing, currently telecommunications in Italy. Good keyboard and telephone skills. PC and Mac experience. Responsible, reliable, enthusiastic, available and willing to move. Contact: Julia Guardi, Viale Monza 126, Milano 20126, Italy. Tel: +39 2 6757508, daytime, +39 2 2553531 evenings.

❷ **DENTIST**, 36, speaking English, French and elementary German, with PhD in Oral Surgery, 5 years' experience as Clinical Assistant in University Department, plus 5 years' experience as Registrar in Hospital Department specialising in treatment of patients with special needs (medically compromised and mentally handicapped) is looking for employment in the private or public sector. Contact: George Stevanis, Karolou Diehl 50 Str., Thessaloniki 546 14, Greece.

LET US HELP YOU FIND A JOB IN EUROPE . . .

Millions of highly skilled people will still be out of work across Europe in 1995. Against this background , more and more highly educated and skilled workers are seeking employment in other European countreis. To reinforce our commitment to you and this market, **The European** is taking action against unemployment by offering FREE advertising to people seeking jobs anywhere in the European Union. Your advertisement will be displayed in lineage form and should include who you are, what skills you have and what languages you speak. In addition, please include a NON-RETURNABLE photograph for us to use with selected advertisements. Your copy should be a maximum of 60 words and will be published in the first available issue, as space permits.

THE EUROPEAN CLASSIFIED ADVERTISEMENT DEPARTMENT

200 Gray's Inn Road, London WC1X8NE
Fax: +44 (0)71 713 1835 Telephone: +44 (0)71 418 7878

. . . SUITED TO YOUR SPECIAL ABILITIES

❸ **MOTIVATED BELGIAN GRADUATE**, 23, BA (University of Leuven) main subject: languages (Dutch, English, French & knowledge of Danish and German). Interested in interpreting, professional journalism or any other job dealing with languages. Computer literate and eager to learn. Contact: Ton Mertens, Oude-Schoolstraat, 9, B-8800 Roeselare, Belgium.

❹ **INTERNATIONAL SALES** and marketing director – British, 40 speaks fluent English and French, and competent Italian. Spent the last 11 years developing international career in both the medical and consumer world. Lived in Netherlands, Belgium and now Switzerland. Seeking a dynamic position that will call upon my excellent leadership and communication skills. Willing to relocate. Contact: N Thornton, Via Selva 2 -CH 6924, Sorengo. Tel: +41 0 91 576134.

Read the four advertisements and write on a piece of paper the following information for each advertisement:

name • skills • languages • work experience • qualifications • job wanted

B Drafting a short text advertising your skills

Work on your own.

Using the newspaper advertisement as a model, write the text that you would send to The European to advertise your skills. Your text should not be longer than sixty words.

C Checking and re-drafting

Work on your own and with a partner.

- Exchange advertisements with your partner.
- Check your partner's advertisement.
- Write any changes you can suggest in pencil.
- Discuss these with your partner.
- Discuss any changes your partner has suggested to your draft.
- Re-draft your advertisement.

Interaction module

In this module you are going to:
- ★ design a new flag.
- ★ describe your new flag.
- ★ draw a flag from another person's description.
- ★ discuss the meaning of a new flag.
- ★ identify some European flags.

The Council of Europe flag dates from 1955. It was adopted by the EEC in 1986. It has got a circle of twelve gold stars on a dark blue background. Each star represents a member country of the European Union.

A Designing a new flag

Work with a partner.

You are going to design a new flag for one of the following:

your town or village • your country • a political party •
a well-known company • a sporting organization

- Discuss the most important things that your flag should represent.
  Try and symbolize some of these things in your new flag.
- Design and draw the flag.
  The design should be simple and easy to draw.
- You should use at least three colours in your design.

B Describing and drawing a flag

Work in groups of four.

You and your partner are going to describe your new flag to the other two people in your group.
As you describe the flag to them, they are going to try and draw it.
Do not show them your design.

When they have finished their drawing, you can correct their mistakes like this:

That's not quite right.
The circle isn't in the right place.
The triangle should be bigger/smaller.
You've put the star in the wrong place. It should be there.
The diagonal lines aren't wide enough.

C Explaining what your new flag represents

Work in groups of four.

Show the other two people in your group your new flag.

Ask and answer questions about the following:
- what the flag represents.
- why they chose those particular colours.
- what the different parts of the flag symbolize.

D European flags

Work in groups of four.

Can you identify the European countries which have these flags?

Listening module

In this module you are going to:

- ★ listen to a traditional Irish story.
- ★ predict what is going to happen in the story.
- ★ identify the correct sequence of events in the story.
- ★ predict how the story is going to end.

A Predicting what is going to happen in the story

Telling stories has played an important part in every culture in the world. In recent years, storytelling in public has become extremely popular again in Europe. You are going to hear an Irish storyteller telling a traditional story to a group of people in a pub.

Work with a partner and in a group of four.

Listen to **Part 1** of the story. The storyteller tells you about one thing and two people that appear in the story. Write their names in the boxes below.

Check your answers with your partner.

Now write down three things that you expect to happen in the story.

I think the ___________ is going to . . .
The ___________ will probably . . .
I expect the ___________ will . . .

Tell the other people in your group what you expect to happen.

B Identifying the correct sequence of events

Work on your own and with a partner.

Read the seven sentences below. The number 1 has been written in one of the boxes. Listen to **Part 2** of the story. Write the numbers 2 to 7 in the boxes to show which sentences come next in the story.

- ❑ He let the little man go.
- ❑ The little man promised not to touch the flower.
- 1 He saw a little man sitting on a stone.
- ❑ The little man took him to a field of flowers.
- ❑ He went home to fetch a spade.
- ❑ He made the little man show him where to find the gold.
- ❑ He tied his handkerchief around the flower.

Check your answers with your partner.

C How is the story going to end?

Work with a partner.

Write two or three sentences to describe what Paddy saw when he got back to the buttercup field with his spade.
Compare your ending to the story with the endings of the other people in your group.

Listen to **Part 3** of the story and see how close your ending was to the actual ending of the story.

Pronunciation module – 1

In this module you are going to:

- ★ listen to and identify two different ways of pronouncing the same word.
- ★ identify the strong pronunciation form used for emphasis.
- ★ practise the two different pronunciations of the strong and weak forms of everyday words.
- ★ write and read aloud a two-line dialogue with examples of strong and weak pronunciation forms of the same word.

A Different ways of pronouncing the same word

Work on your own and with a partner.

You probably know that the word THE can be said in two different ways.
Listen to the model sentence. Now listen to the eight examples.
Write a tick in the box if the pronunciation of the word THE is the same as in the model sentence, and a cross if it is different.

1 ❑ THE BOOK
2 ❑ THE TREE
3 ❑ THE END
4 ❑ THE NEWS
5 ❑ THE OFFICE
6 ❑ THE UNDERGROUND
7 ❑ THE PIANO
8 ❑ THE INFORMATION

Check your answer with a partner and discuss how the pronunciation of the word THE depends on the first sound in the word that comes after it.

The two different ways of pronouncing the word are called the *strong form* and the *weak form*.

Listen to the next part of the tape. In the first four examples you will hear the *strong form* /iː/ of THE followed by four examples of the *weak form* /ə/.

B The strong form of pronunciation for emphasis

Work on your own and with a partner.

The strong form is also used for emphasis. Listen to the two different ways of saying the same sentence.

You will hear this sentence four times:
"It's the most important scientific discovery this century."

Write the letter S next to the numbers below when the strong form of THE is used for emphasis.

1 ____________________
2 ____________________
3 ____________________
4 ____________________

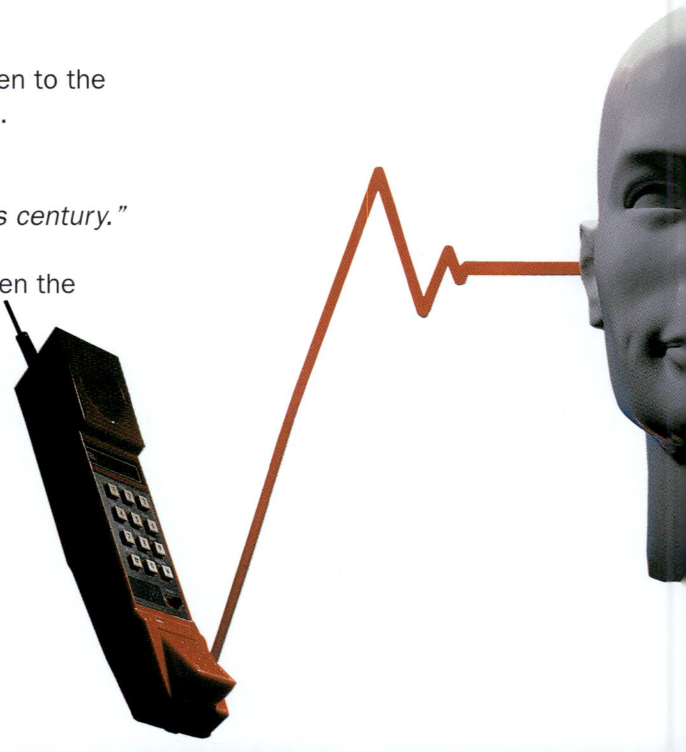

C Weak and strong pronunciation

Work with a partner.

You are going to hear someone reading the sentences below.
Listen to the tape and decide which sentence has the *strong form* of each of the following words: A; AN; AND; AT; OF; AS.
The *weak forms* all have the same sound as the weak form of THE /ə/
Practise saying the sentences aloud exactly as they are said on the tape.
Ask your partner to listen to you and tell you if you make a mistake.

A	Once a week.
	I said a small cup, not two small cups.
AN	It's an old photograph.
	I said you could have an orange, not two!
AND	It's black and white.
	She can speak French, German, English, Italian, Spanish and Russian.
AT	I saw him at six o' clock, not after six o' clock.
	I'm going to Paris at the weekend.
OF	Two cups of tea, please.
	No, I didn't say "odd", I said "of".
AS	His hands were as cold as ice.
	What's the difference between "as" and "like"?

Now you are going to hear each of the following words used in two sentences:

can • was • than • for • from • to

In the first sentence, you will hear the *weak* pronunciation of the word. In the second sentence you will hear the *strong* pronunciation. Listen and repeat each sentence. In everyday English, the weak pronunciation of all of these words is used more often than the strong pronunciation.

D Strong and weak pronunciation forms of the same word

Work on your own and with a partner.
Listen to the conversations.

Each of the sentences below is one part of a conversation between two people. The second person uses the *strong* pronunciation form of the word in bold type to correct, check or disagree with the first person.

Write the missing part of the conversation.
Read the conversations aloud with your partner.

1	1ST PERSON	______________________
	2ND PERSON	Women **can** play football!
2	1ST PERSON	______________________
	2ND PERSON	It **was** real gold; I saw it with my own eyes!
3	1ST PERSON	______________________
	2ND PERSON	Did you say "**than**" or "then"?
4	1ST PERSON	______________________
	2ND PERSON	They said "**for**" not "fur".
5	1ST PERSON	______________________
	2ND PERSON	They're coming **from** the airport not to the airport.
6	1ST PERSON	______________________
	2ND PERSON	She wrote a letter **to** Jane, not about Jane.

Pronunciation module – 2

In this module you are going to:
- ★ identify the sounds that are linked in fluent speech.
- ★ practise linking the sounds in the same way as a fluent speaker.
- ★ practise linking a word which ends with a vowel sound and a word which begins with a vowel sound using the extra sounds /w/ and /j/.

A Sounds that are linked together in fluent speech

Work on your own and with a partner.
Listen to two people reading these sentences.

If I had left an hour earlier, I would have had plenty of time.
If I hadn't had lunch with Alison, I could have left earlier.

Which person sounds more natural and fluent?
What is the reason for this?
Discuss your opinion with your partner.

Listen to the fluent speaker reading the first sentence again.

If‿I had left‿an‿hour‿earlier‿I would have had plenty‿of time.

Notice how some sounds are linked together.

Now listen to the fluent speaker reading the second sentence.
Draw a line between the two words where the final sound of one word runs into the first sound of the next word.

If I hadn't had lunch with Alison, I could have left earlier.

Check your answers with your partner.

B Joining the consonant and vowel sounds at the end and beginning of words

Work with a partner.

Read the two sentences aloud. Ask your partner to listen to you and check that you are joining the sounds in the same way as the fluent speaker. The final sound in one word is normally linked with the first sound in the next word when one word ends with a consonant sound and the next word begins with a vowel sound, for example:

Please, come‿in – They don't like‿it

Draw a line between the two words where the final sound of one word runs into the first sound of the next word.

She works on Saturday and Sunday.
They live in an old house in the country.
They always come between six and seven o'clock.
I think it's too much for us.

Check your answers with your partner. Listen to the sentences on the tape. Practise reading the sentences aloud. Remember not to stress the linking sounds too much.

C Linking two vowel sounds with the sounds /w/ and /j/

Work on your own and with a partner. Listen to the following sentences on the tape.

Do‿I need my passport? Don't go‿out yet! Who‿are you talking to?

In order to link the following pairs of words – Do‿I, Go‿out, Who‿are – the speaker adds the sound /w/ between the two vowel sounds. This makes it possible to say the two sounds without making a break between them.

Listen to the tape again and practise saying the sentences aloud to your partner as fluently as possible. Remember not to stress the linking sounds too much.

Linking two vowel sounds with the sound /j/. Listen to the following sentences on the tape.

We‿always say, "Hello!" I didn't like the‿evening meal. Would you like tea‿or coffee?

In order to link the following pairs of words – We‿always, the‿evening, tea‿or – the speaker adds the sound /j/ between the two vowel sounds. This makes it possible to say the two sounds without making a break between them.

Listen to the tape again and practise saying the sentences aloud to your partner as fluently as possible. Remember not to stress the linking sounds too much.

Vocabulary module – 1

In this module you are going to:

- ★ sort words connected with transport into categories.
- ★ match pairs of words connected with transport.
- ★ revise some words connected with the weather.
- ★ match some weather adjectives and nouns.
- ★ re-construct a poem.

A Words in categories

Work on your own.

Select the words from this list that are connected with travelling by rail, road, sea and air, and on a piece of paper write them in the correct column.

plane • egg • knee • train • ferry • guitar • lorry • orange • toothpaste • tube • bus • leaf • coach • motorbike • taxes • taxi • jumbo jet • elephant • tram • bicycle • boot • yacht • locomotive • shuffle • hovercraft • van • lake • rose • underground • ice • elbow • ship • car

BY RAIL	BY ROAD	BY SEA	BY AIR

B Words which are often used together

Work in pairs.

In every language you find pairs or groups of words that are frequently used together. Which words from Group A are frequently used with words from Group B? Try and find ten pairs of words. You can use some words several times.

Group A
business • railway • tourist • ferry • single • freight • passenger • return • first • air

Group B
information • steward/-ess • waggon • journey • station • fare • train • class • ticket • terminal

C Words connected with the weather

Work on your own.

Can you find twelve words connected with **WEATHER** in the square of letters below?

Here are some clues to help you:
- two words begin with the letter **W**
- three words begin with the letter **C**
- three letters begin with the letter **S**
- each of the other words begin with one of these letters: **F-H-T-R**

C	B	V	D	H	E	G	T	V	R	S	C
B	O	C	H	U	A	Z	E	D	A	C	O
L	K	X	O	A	H	W	M	E	I	W	Z
B	E	S	T	O	R	M	P	D	N	X	R
W	B	O	O	T	S	M	E	J	W	U	K
X	Q	G	Y	H	N	D	R	Y	I	Q	Y
C	J	B	D	F	O	G	A	E	N	W	D
L	E	U	S	T	W	E	T	C	D	K	N
P	T	D	D	C	L	O	U	D	Y	O	R
V	Y	C	D	O	X	J	R	E	B	P	V
K	O	G	C	O	L	D	E	N	I	G	E
P	O	G	S	L	B	G	S	U	N	N	Y

Sort these words into pairs with opposite meanings.

freezing • clear • dull • boiling • calm • bright • rough • cloudy

Which could be used to describe:
the sky • the sea • the temperature?

Work with a partner.

Using the words below, fill in the gaps in this short poem by the English writer, *Hilaire Belloc (1870-1953).*

left • goodnight • sister • moon • other • morning • dawn • brother

The early morning

The __________ on the one hand, the dawn on the __________.
The moon is my __________, the __________ is my __________.
The moon on my __________ and the dawn on my right,
My brother, good __________: my sister, __________.

Vocabulary module – 2

In this module you are going to:

- ★ match people's occupations with what they often say at work.
- ★ match people's occupations with the places where they work and the objects they use at work.
- ★ find out someone's job by asking questions.

A Matching typical phrases with occupations

Work on your own and with a partner.

Which of the following people might say this while doing their job? Write the correct number in the box.

a doctor ❑	a flight attendant ❑	a actor ❑	a porter ❑
a chemist ❑	a policewoman ❑	a dentist ❑	a lawyer ❑

1 *To be, or not to be – that is the question . . . .*
2 *Your tablets will be ready in twenty minutes.*
3 *Open your mouth wide please.*
4 *Have you had the pain in your chest for a long time?*
5 *My client is not guilty of stealing the money.*
6 *Could I see your driving licence, please?*
7 *Will all passengers please fasten their seat belts.*
8 *Are these your suitcases too, madam?*

Check your answers with your partner.

B Matching places of work and objects with occupations

Work on your own and with a partner.

Who works here?

- in a restaurant __________
- in a hospital __________
- in a kitchen __________
- in a court of law __________
- in a school __________
- in a shop __________
- in a laboratory __________
- in an office __________
- in a hotel __________

Write the name of the occupation next to the place above. Check your answers with your partner.

Work on your own and with a partner.

Match the names of the following objects with the correct picture.

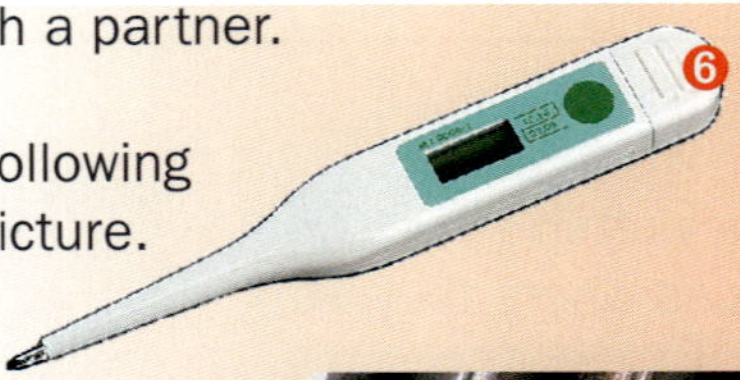

- a pair of scissors ❑
- a menu ❑
- a saucepan ❑
- a thermometer ❑
- a notebook ❑
- a test tube ❑
- a shovel ❑
- a screwdriver ❑

Now match the objects with the people who normally use them at work.

a	a workman	❑ 3	a pair of scissors
b	an electrician	❑	a menu
c	a scientist	❑	a saucepan
d	a waitress	❑	a thermometer
e	a nurse	❑	a notebook
f	a hairdresser	❑	a test tube
g	a cook	❑	a shovel
h	a policeman	❑	a screwdriver

Check your answers with your partner.

C Finding out someone's job

Work in groups of four.

Each person in the group chooses one job or profession from the lists above. The other people in the group must guess what the job or profession is. They can ask five questions each. The person answering the questions can only answer with the following words:
YES/NO/SOMETIMES/IT DEPENDS.

Here are some questions you may want to ask.

- *Do you work indoors?*
- *Do you need special training to do your job?*
- *Do you use special equipment when you do your job?*
- *Do you work with other people?*
- *Do you work in a kitchen?*

Record Chart Block Two Session 9 – 16

At the end of each session, record what you have done.

			From the Module Banks
Session 9	Grammar ❑ conditionals	Interaction ❑ Plans	________ ❑ ________
Session 10	Grammar ❑ ________	Writing ❑ ________	________ ❑ ________
Session 11	Listening ❑ ________	Grammar ❑ ________	________ ❑ ________
Session 12	Grammar ❑ ________	Reading ❑ ________	________ ❑ ________
Session 13	Grammar ❑ ________	Interaction ❑ ________	________ ❑ ________
Session 14	Grammar ❑ ________	Writing ❑ ________	________ ❑ ________
Session 15	Reading ❑ ________	Grammar ❑ ________	________ ❑ ________
Session 16	Grammar ❑ ________	Listening ❑ ________	________ ❑ ________

Evaluation Chart Block Two Session 9 – 16

Now that you have finished this block, think back over the work you have done in each area.

Which modules did you find easiest? Which hardest? Which areas do you need to concentrate on in your future work in English?

Fill in this chart to show how you feel about your performance in the seven areas covered by English for Europe. **This is your chart, for you.**

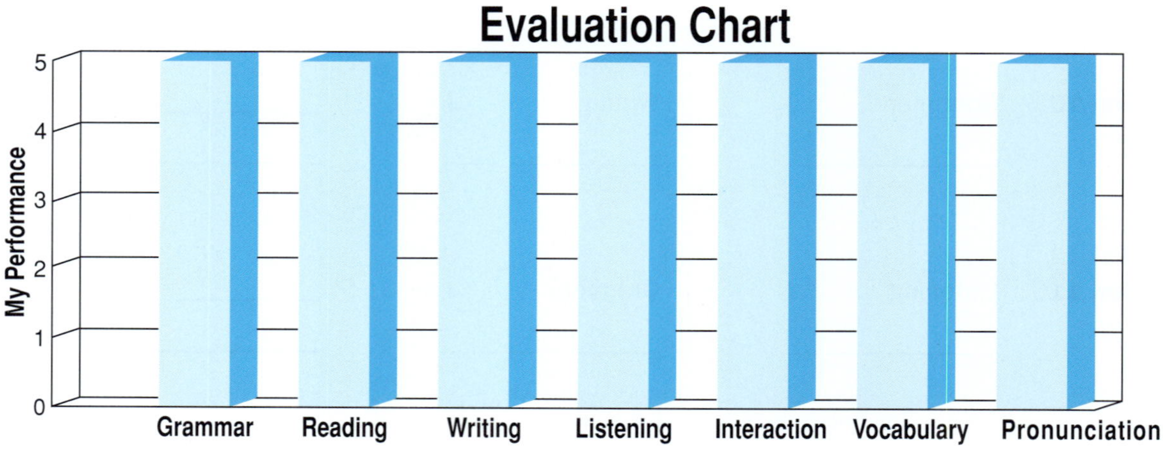

In each area, fill in the chart up to the number which you feel matches your performance.

Grammar

5 I knew all this already.
3 I knew some of this, but there was quite a lot of new material.
1 Nearly all the grammar we covered was new for me.

Reading & Listening

5 I understood everything.
3 I understood enough to answer the questions.
1 I didn't understand very much at all.

Writing

5 I can write what I want to say quite easily and without too many mistakes.
3 I know that my writing has some mistakes, but people can understand what I write.
1 I don't feel confident about writing in English. I find it hard.

Interaction

5 I can express what I want to say quite easily and without too many mistakes.
3 I know that when I speak English I make some mistakes, but people can understand what I say.
1 I don't feel confident about speaking English. I find it hard.

Vocabulary

5 I knew all this already.
3 I knew some of this, but there was quite a lot of new material.
1 Nearly all the vocabulary we covered was new for me.

Pronunciation

5 I think my accent in English is quite good.
3 I find some sounds in English quite difficult, but people can understand me.
1 I have a lot of problems with English pronunciation.

Welcome to Block Three Session 17 – 24

This block consists of eight 90-minute sessions each of which consists of one prescribed module and two chosen from the Block Three Module Banks.

There is an overview of what you will find in this block on page 104.

Each session in this block has two "free slots" into which modules from the Block Three Module Banks can be fitted.

This allows the group (learners and teacher) to shape each lesson to a considerable extent according to their preferences.

Decisions about the module to be covered in each session can be made during the lesson or in advance, according to the wishes and interests of the group.

Modules from any area can be selected in any session. But we recommend variety. It is not usually a good idea to do two modules from the same area in one session. And it is not usually a good idea to do two modules from the same areas in successive sessions.

Within each area, you should do modules **A**, **B** and **C** in that order.

Remember that follow-up material for each module is available in the Learner's Book.

Block Three Overview Sessions 17 – 24

Prescribed Modules

17	**Grammar** questions & question tags
18	**Grammar** past tense forms
19	**Grammar** ***may***, ***might***, ***could*** ***if*** and ***unless***
20	**Grammar** indefinite & definite articles
21	**Grammar** present perfect continuons; ***since/for*** with negatives
22	**Grammar** modals with the perfect
23	**Grammar** review of all passive verb forms
24	**Grammar** review of language from this Block

Module Banks

Grammar module questions and question tags

In this module you are going to:
- ★ look at some examples of three similar grammar points in action.
- ★ practise using these grammar points in your situation.

A Checking

Ana is in Lyon. She is talking to Pierre Dutronc about his holiday plans. They talked briefly about this last time she was in Lyon, but she is checking that she remembers correctly.

You're going to Portugal this year, aren't you.
Yes. that's right, we are.
Aren't you going camping.
Yes, that's right. We're hiring a tent.
You aren't taking your dog with you, are you.
No we aren't. He's too old to travel all that way.

Work in groups of three.

Check with your partners some information about their families, their work, their hobbies or their holidays.

B Reminding

Maria's daughter is going to take her driving test. Maria is reminding her what to do.

Don't forget to take your glasses, will you.
No, I won't.
Remember to look in the mirror before you start, won't you. Yes, I will.
Don't drive through a red light, will you.
No, of course I won't.
Drive carefully, won't you. Yes, of course I will.

Work in groups of three.

One member of the group is leaving next week for a trip to the jungles of Brazil. What do you need to remind your colleague to do (or not to do)?

C Complaining

Antje is now working for another manager as well as for Ana. She has so much to do that sometimes things are late. When this happens, the other manager always complains.

Isn't that report I gave you yesterday ready yet?	*– No, I'm afraid it isn't.*
Aren't the figures for last week ready yet?	*– No, I'm afraid they aren't.*
Haven't you finished the sales forecasts yet?	*– No, I'm afraid I haven't.*
Didn't you make that reservation for me yesterday?	*– No, I'm afraid I didn't.*

Work in groups of three.

One member of the group thinks of a situation (e. g. in a shop, in a hotel, in a restaurant). The other members must think of a complaint to go in the situation using language like this.

Module Banks

To complete your work in this session, choose modules from two of the Block Three Module Banks. You can do modules from any of the banks according to your choice.

Modules inside each bank should be covered in order.

When you have finished the session, complete the Record Chart on page 150.

Grammar module past tense forms

In this module you are going to:

- ★ look at some examples of three similar grammar points in action.
- ★ practise using these grammar points in your situation.

A Being polite

Maria Cellini has a new secretary. Look at the way she asks and offers to do things.

Ms Cellini, I was wondering if I could leave early on Friday afternoon.
I wanted to ask you if I could take a few days off at the end of the month.
Would you like me to make another copy of the report?
Did you want me to book a flight to Brussels for you?

Work in groups of three.

An official delegation from your twin town is visiting your region and you are helping to arrange their programme. What might you ask or offer the leader of the delegation?

B Describing an awful experience

Last week Alison went out for a meal. She did not enjoy it.

The soup tasted as if it was burnt.
The music sounded as if the band was drunk.

Work in groups of three.

Can you make some more sentences about Alison's meal? Here are some words you can use.

felt • looked • smelt • sounded • tasted + as if

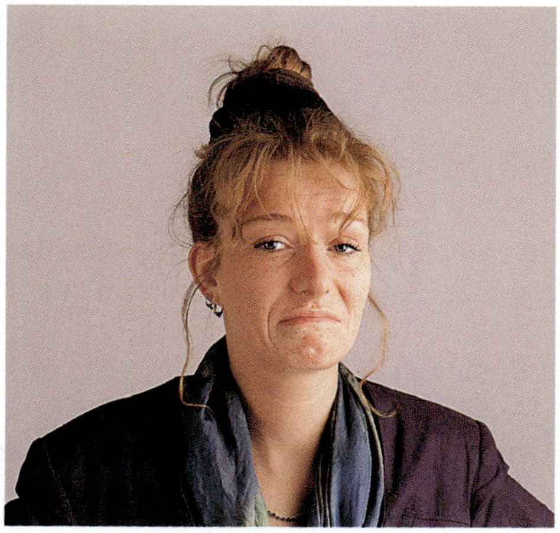

C Wishing . . .

Ana has travelled all over Europe to prepare her new brochure. Now she is sitting at home looking back over the experience.

I wish I could speak more languages.
I wish I had more time to get to know some of the people I met better.
I wish I didn't have to produce the brochure so quickly.

Work in groups of three.

What would you change about this book?
Or about the English language?

Module Banks

To complete your work in this session, choose modules from two of the Block Three Module Banks. You can do modules from any of the banks according to your choice.

Modules inside each bank should be covered in order.

When you have finished the session, complete the Record Chart on page 150.

Grammar module – may, might, could; if and unless

In this module you are going to:

- ★ look at some examples of three similar grammar points in action.
- ★ practise using these grammar points in your situation.

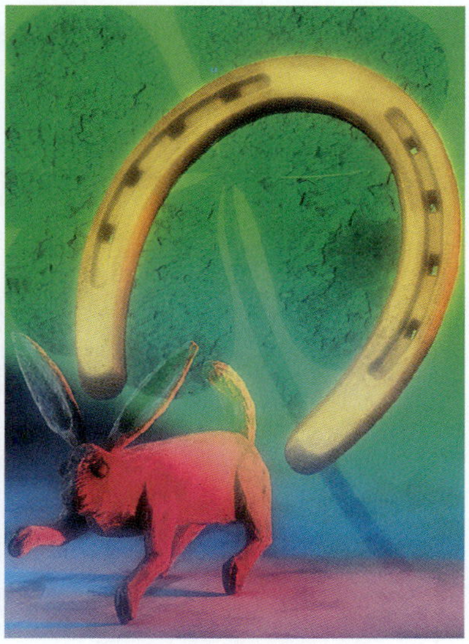

A Expressing universal laws

Look at these examples. Some things are the same all over Europe – and all over the world.

If you eat too much, you put on weight.
If you have twelve socks in your drawer, you can never find a matching pair.
If you wash your car, it starts to rain.

Work in groups of three.

What are the universal laws of everyday life in your experience?

B Looking at *may, might, could*

Earlier (on page 53) you practised some sentences about environmental problems.

If the amount of pollution in the Rhine continues to rise, all the plant and animal life in the river will/might *be destroyed.*

Work in groups of three.

What is the difference between *will* be destroyed and *might* be destroyed?

Look at this:
If the amount of pollution in the Rhine continues to rise, all the plant and animal life in the river may/could *be destroyed.*

What is the difference here?

Look at some of the sentences you made on page 53. Which fits better: *will*, *may*, *might* or *could*?

C Using *unless*

Ana is beginning to worry about the brochure she is producing.

Unless I get the photographs this week, I'll miss the printing deadline.
Unless I interview two more people, I won't have enough material.
I might not finish in time, unless I work all weekend.

Work in groups of three.

Make some sentences like these about the political situation at the moment in your region, in your country or in Europe.

Module Banks

To complete your work in this session, choose modules from two of the Block Three Module Banks. You can do modules from any of the banks according to your choice.

Modules inside each bank should be covered in order.

When you have finished the session, complete the Record Chart on page 150.

Grammar module uses of the indefinite and definite article

In this module you are going to:

- ★ look at some examples of three similar grammar points in action.
- ★ practise using these grammar points in your situation.

A Asking about times

Look at this table of flight times.

Work in groups of three.

Ask each other how long it takes to fly from Paris to different places on the chart – and to other places.

In the answer use these phrases:

half an hour • an hour and a half/one and a half hours • two/three and a half hours

From Paris to . . .	
. . . London	30 minutes
. . . Barcelona	90 minutes
. . . Warsaw	150 minutes
. . . Tel Aviv	210 minutes

B Describing people and places

Sometimes it is useful to describe people and places like this.

As a teacher he is hopeless, but as a friend I like him a lot.
As a place to spend a romantic weekend it is wonderful, but as a place to live it would be rather boring.

Work in groups of three.

One member of the group thinks of a person or a place and describes it in the way set out above. The others try to guess who or where they are describing.

C Giving opinions

People often have different opinions about things.

Holidays?

The longer, the better.
The more exotic, the better.
The less stressful, the better.
The more I have, the more I want.
The longer they are, the harder it is to go back to work.

Work in groups of three.

Try to make some sentences like these to give your opinion about the followings:

cars • recipes • hobbies • travel • houses

Module Banks

To complete your work in this session, choose modules from two of the Block Three Module Banks. You can do modules from any of the banks according to your choice.

Modules inside each bank should be covered in order.

When you have finished the session, complete the Record Chart on page 150.

Grammar module the present perfect continuous

In this module you are going to:
- ★ look at some examples of this grammar point in action.
- ★ practise using this grammar point in your situation.

A Grammar in action

Earlier (on page 75) you met Martina Dege, Francoise Duclerc and Paolo Rezzi.
Which of these sentences goes with which of them?

1 *. . . has been working for INTEX for four years.*
2 *. . . has been working for INTEX for fifteen years.*
3 *. . . has been living in Lyon for two years.*

Look at the way we find out this information.

How long has Martina been working for INTEX?
How long have you been living in Lyon?

And the way we give information:

for two years • for ten years • for six months • for three weeks
since last year • since Christmas • since March • since last weekend

B What is going on?

Work in groups of three.
Can you make a "rule" to explain the difference between:
I have lived in Como all my life.
I have been living in Lyon for two years.

And between the use of since and the use of for in sentences like these?

C Practising the rules

Work in groups of three.

Since or for? Test each other.

ten days • a fortnight • last Easter • 15th December • Christmas 1994 •
three weeks • six months • two and a half years

Make up some more.

Now look at these six sentences. One person picks a number.
One person asks *how long . . .* . The third person gives an answer.
Take turns.

1 Paolo is feeling depressed.
2 Antje likes rock 'n roll.
3 Franzi and Dennis are living together again.
4 Ana and Ralf are married.
5 Maria's daughter is learning to drive.
6 It's snowing!

Module Banks

To complete your work in this session, choose modules from two of the Block Three Module Banks. You can do modules from any of the banks according to your choice.

Modules inside each bank should be covered in order.

When you have finished the session, complete the Record Chart on page 150.

Grammar module modals with the perfect

In this module you are going to:

- ★ look at some examples of three similar grammar points in action.
- ★ practise using these grammar points in your situation.

A Talking about possibilities

Is Frank the most boring person in Europe?

I could have gone to Italy last year, but I decided to stay at home.
I could have got a job as a space engineer, but I decided to stay here in the office.
I could have bought a Porsche but I decided to keep my Opel Kadett.

Work in groups of three.

What would the most boring person you know say?

B Supposing . . .

Look at these examples.

I spent last night in the bar with Frank.
That must have been very interesting!

Maria's daughter has passed her driving test.
She must have practised a lot.

Mart spent a year in the Lyon office after he finished training at home in Holland.
He must have found it very strange at first.

Work in groups of three.

Can you make some more exchanges like these, perhaps about characters from English for Europe, perhaps about politicians, perhaps about people in the news at the moment.

C Using conditionals: *certainty, possibility, ability*

Look at these examples.

If Ana hadn't visited Alison, she wouldn't have seen Gloucester.
If she had left Gloucester earlier, she might/could have avoided the traffic jam.
If she had avoided the traffic jam, she could have caught the ferry.

Work in groups of three.

Which of these examples deals with ***certainty***, which with ***possibility*** and which with ***ability***?

Can you make some more sentences of each type, perhaps about the same characters you talked about in the last section.

Module Banks

To complete your work in this session, choose modules from two of the Block Three Module Banks. You can do modules from any of the banks according to your choice.

Modules inside each bank should be covered in order.

When you have finished the session, complete the Record Chart on page 150.

Grammar module the passive

In this module you are going to:

- ★ look at some examples of three similar grammar points in action.
- ★ practise using these grammar points in a range of situations.

A The news

Look at this news item.

An Airbus of the new European company Fanair crashed this morning as it was coming in to land at Manchester airport. All ninety-one passengers and crew were killed. Relatives are being informed as quickly as possible and further details will be given later. Meanwhile, all flights from Manchester have been cancelled. First reports say the plane may have been hit by lightning but this has not yet been confirmed.

B Who did it?

Work in groups of three.

- Who killed the passengers and crew?
- Who is informing the relatives?
- Who will give the further details later?
- Who has cancelled the flights from Manchester?
- Who has not yet confirmed the reports about lightning?

Do we know who did it? If we do, is it important? How does this influence the way the language is used?

- What may have hit the plane?
- Why does the news report not say "First reports say that lightning may have hit the plane . . . ."

C What is going on?

Look at these examples.

The weather is awful and Doris still hasn't arrived.

Her flight must have been delayed by the storms.

We're not going tomorrow, we're going next month.

Our trip has been postponed.

Work in groups of three.

Make up similar "explanations" for these. Will you use a *by* phrase or not?

We can't celebrate yet. (order not confirmed)
There was no electricity in the flat. (bill not paid)
The villagers of San Cristóbal are very happy. (new by-pass built)
It's really cold in here. (heating switched off)
When I saw them last night they were feeling very upset. (cat run over)

Can you think of any other "explanations"?

Module Banks

To complete your work in this session, choose modules from two of the Block Three Module Banks. You can do modules from any of the banks according to your choice.

Modules inside each bank should be covered in order.

When you have finished the session, complete the Record Chart on page 150.

Grammar module – review

In this module you are going to:
- ★ review the grammar points from this Block of English for Europe.
- ★ practise using some of these grammar points in a text.

1 Questions and question tags

Checking
- *You're going to Portugal this year, aren't you. Yes. that's right, we are.*
- *Aren't you going camping. Yes, that's right. We're hiring a tent.*
- *You aren't taking your dog with you, are you. No we aren't. He's too old to travel all that way.*

Reminding
- *Don't forget to take your driving licence, will you. No, I won't.*
- *Remember to look in the mirror before you start, won't you. Yes, I will.*
- *Don't drive through a red light, will you. No, of course I won't.*
- *Drive carefully, won't you. Yes, of course I will.*

Complaining
- *Isn't that report I gave you yesterday ready yet?*
- *Aren't the figures for last week ready yet?*
- *Haven't you finished the sales forecasts yet?*
- *Didn't you make that reservation for me yesterday?*

2 Past tense forms

Being polite
- *Ms Cellini, I was wondering if I could leave early on Friday afternoon.*
- *I wanted to ask you if I could take a few days off at the end of the month.*
- *Would you like me to make another copy of the report?*
- *Did you want me to book a flight to Brussels for you?*

Describing an awful experience
- *The soup tasted as if it was burnt.*
- *The music sounded as if the band was drunk.*

Wishing . . .
- *I wish I could speak more languages.*
- *I wish I had more time to get to know some of the people I met better.*
- *I wish I didn't have to produce the brochure so quickly.*

3 Expressing universal laws

Universal laws
- *If you eat too much, you put on weight.*
- *If you have twelve socks in your drawer, you can never find a matching pair.*
- *If you wash your car, it starts to rain.*

Looking at *may, might, could*
- *If the amount of pollution in the Rhine continues to rise, all the plant and animal life in the river may/might/could be destroyed.*

Using *unless*
- *Unless I get the photographs this week, I'll miss the printing deadline.*
- *Unless I interview two more people, I won't have enough material.*
- *I might not finish in time, unless I work all weekend.*

4 The indefinite and definite article

Asking about times
- *half an hour; an hour and a half/one and a half hours; two/three and a half hours*

Describing people and places
- *As a teacher he is hopeless, but as a friend I like him a lot.*
- *As a place to spend a romantic weekend it is wonderful, but as a place to live it would be rather boring.*

Giving opinions
Holidays? *The longer, the better.*
The more exotic, the better.
The less stressful, the better.
The more I have, the more I want.
The longer they are, the harder it is to go back to work.

5 The present perfect continuous

- *How long has Martina been working for INTEX?*

for two years • for ten years • for six months • for three weeks
since last year • since Christmas • since March • since last weekend

- *I have lived in Como all my life.*
- *I have been living in Lyon for two years.*

6 Modals with the perfect

Talking about possibilities

– *I could have gone to Italy last year, but I decided to stay at home.*

Supposing

– *I spent last night in the bar with Frank.*
That must have been very interesting!

Using conditionals: *certainty, possibility, ability*

– *If Ana hadn't visited Alison, she wouldn't have seen Gloucester.*
– *If she had left Gloucester earlier, she might/could have avoided the traffic jam.*
– *If she had avoided the traffic jam, she could have caught the ferry.*

7 The passive

– *Her flight must have been delayed by the storms.*
– *Our trip has been postponed.*

Text completion

Work in groups of three.

Find the best word or words to complete the blanks in this text. Use the words in brackets to help you.

Language skills are the key to success

Across Europe people (realise) ______________[1] that mastery of languages is a key to (improve) ______________[2] their career prospects, to cross-border travel, and to better communication with fellow-Europeans.

Johanna Wilson, a Scottish teacher of English living in France, began studying German so that she (can) ____________[3] take part in a German exchange programme a year ago.

"If I (not study) ______________[4] the language, I (not enjoy) ______________[5] the visit," she said. Unless you (can understand) ______________[6] what is happening, you (always feel) ______________[7] an outsider. But I really enjoyed the feeling of (break) ______________[8] down the barriers."

Johanna (now study) ______________[9] German for (2 ½) ______________[10] years. She (plan) ______________[11] to start learning Italian soon. Recently she (be offer) ______________[12] a job in Turin but she did not take it.

"I did not take the job because as ______________[13] place to live, I thought Turin was too hectic. I'm looking for somewhere a bit quieter - and maybe even hotter, (hotter/better) ______________[14] But in a way I wish I (accept) ______________[15] the job in Turin. It (force) ______________[16] me to start learning the language. If you (not have) ______________[17] that focus, you have to be really motivated to keep going to classes, ______________[18]?"

That motivation (often provide) ______________[19] by the desire for a better job. Jean-Mark Recour of IRD Consultants says that in the job market nowadays language skills are ______________[20] important as computer skills.

Module Banks

To complete your work in this session, choose modules from two of the Block Three Module Banks. You can do modules from any of the banks according to your choice.

Modules inside each bank should be covered in order.

When you have finished the session, complete the Record Chart on page 150.

Now that you have finished English for Europe, complete the Evaluation Chart on page 151.

Block Three Module Banks

Reading module – 1

In this module you are going to:

★ match the names of different tools with the correct pictures.
★ read a text from the business section of a newspaper and match topic sentences with the correct paragraphs.

A Matching the names of different tools with the correct pictures

Work on your own and with a partner.

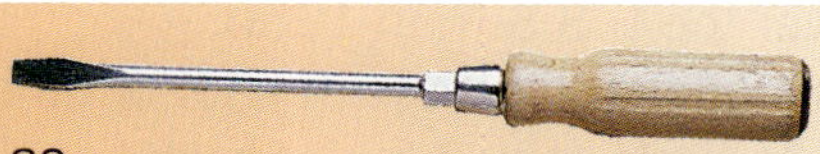

The Swiss Army knife is a Swiss product that is as well-known throughout the world as the Swatch wrist watch and the Toblerone chocolate bar. One of the reasons for its success is the clever design which combines up to thirty-one different tools in a small space.

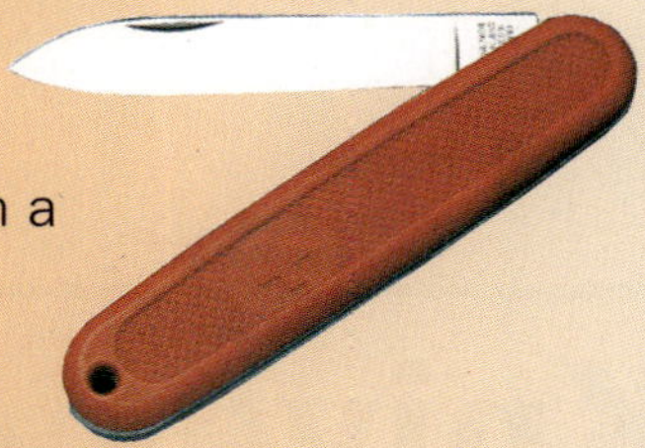

Here are pictures of some of the tools you can find in a Swiss Army knife.

Match the words with the pictures.

a penknife • a nail file • a pair of scissors • a saw •
a corkscrew • a tin opener • a bottle opener •
a screwdriver • a pair of tweezers

Check your answers with your partner.

B Matching topic sentences with paragraphs

Work on your own and with a partner.

A topic sentence tries to express the main idea in a paragraph as simply as possible. Read the list of topic sentences (1 – 14) on page 124/125, and check the meaning of any words which you do not understand.

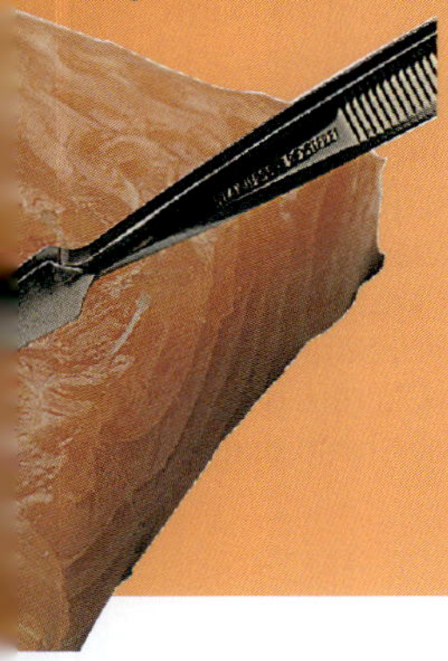

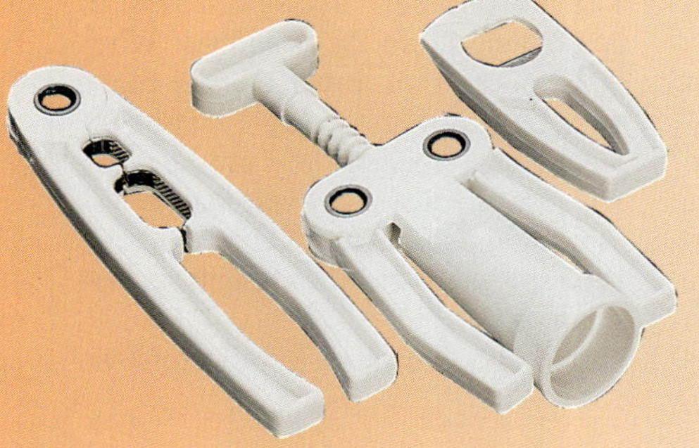

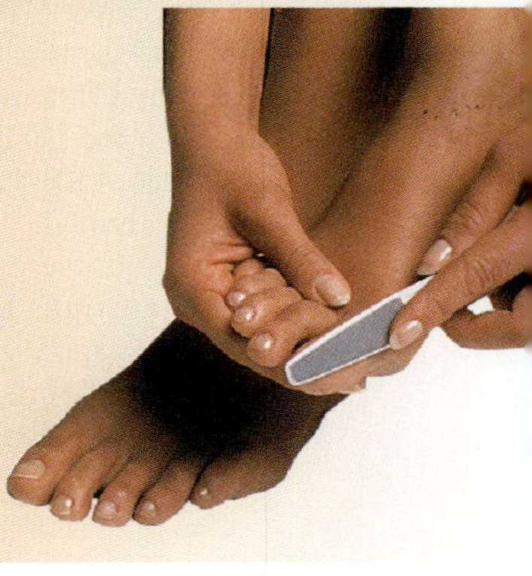

Now read the newspaper article and write the number of the **topic sentence** next to the correct paragraph in the text.

1 Karl Elsener made the first Swiss Army knife in 1891.
2 The Swiss Army does not use knives with red handles.
3 Chinese copies of the knife with the red handle are 25% cheaper in the U.S. than the original knives made only by the Swiss companies Victorinox and Wenger.
4 The Swiss Army knife is sold all over the world.
5 Gary Powers, a U.S. Air Force pilot, was carrying a Swiss Army knife when his spy plane was shot down over the U.S.S.R. in 1960.
6 Victorinox and Wenger have spent a lot of time and money fighting legal battles against companies who have copied their design.

THE EURO
THE WEEKLY NEW

Knives drawn in battle

John Parry
reports on Chinese copies of a national symbol

THERE is a Swiss Army bicycle, there is a Swiss Army watch – although nobody seems very clear as to whether these articles are actually used by the Swiss Army.But the item that catches the world's attention, and which is now the subject of a legal battle with China, is the Swiss Army knife.

Made by only two companies in Switzerland, Victorinox in Ibach and Wenger in Delemont, the redhandled knife has become as much a symbol of Switzerland as the Alps. Now it is threatened by Chinese-made imitations, which sell in the United States for less than a quarter of the Swiss price.

Victorinox, through its US distributor, has taken the Chinese to court claiming they have no right to use the words "Swiss Army" and the white cross on a red background flag on their knives. Victorinox's US distributor does not expect a final decision for months yet.

Actually the red knives made by Victorinox and sold worldwide are a misnomer. The knives it supplies to the Swiss Army itself are different – for one thing the army specifies that no paint be used on the knives supplied to it.

For another, there is no corkscrew. The "commercial" knife not only has a corkscrew but a can opener, a screwdriver and many more gadgets as well.

The knife itself always seems to be popping up in the headlines. When the Soviets shot down U2 spy plane pilot Gary Powers in 1960, one of the pieces of evidence they produced to show that he was a spy was that he was carrying a Swiss Army knife. Who else but a spy would carry such sophisticated equipment?

Former US President Lindon Johnson used to hand out Swiss Army knives with LBJ engraved on them to guests at the White House. And Nasa has ordered it as standard equipment for the Columbia programme.

The knives are sold in more than 100 countries, with the largest numbers of customers in the US and Germany.

All this commercial activity stems from the return to Switzerland in 1884 of Karl Elsener, a young Swiss who had emigrated from Ibach, near Schwyz, to learn the trade of cutler in Germany. In 1891, seven years after setting up his own business, he persuaded the Swiss Army – which until then had bought its knives in Germany – to buy a domestic product. The Swiss Army knife was born.

The original design, however, was heavy so Elsener invented a lighter and more elegant knife with only two springs for its six blades.

The Swiss Army knife now comes in 100 different combinations. The main model is the SwissChamp, which has 31 options and is so aesthetic that the New

7 The Swiss Army does not use knives with corkscrews.
8 There are almost 1,000 employees in the Victorinox company.
9 There is a legal battle between the Swiss and the Chinese about the Swiss Army knife.
10 Karl Elsener changed the design of the knife.
11 Victorinox has taken the Chinese manufacturers to court.
12 The company founded by Karl Elsener is called Victorinox.
13 The Swiss Army knife has been used as a present by a U.S. president and as standard equipment by NASA.
14 One of the many models of the Swiss Army knife has won a design award.

Check your answers with your partner.

PEAN

APER FOR EUROPE

over Swiss Army fakes

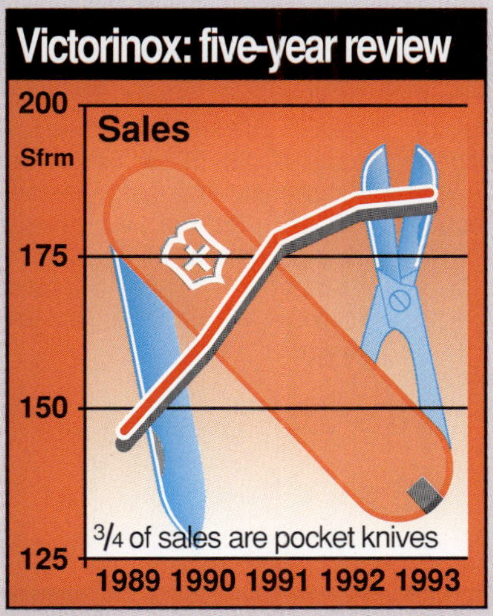

York Museum of Modern Art has given it an award for Good Industrial Design. The Victorinox company is named after Victoria, the mother of founder Elsener, whose name is combined with the world Inox from *inoxydable* (stainless in French). In fact, the varieties of Swiss Army knife are not the largest part of Victorinox's production.

The company employs 975 people in an area of Switzerland notable for farming. Presiding over this enterprise is Carl Elsener Jr, the chief executive officer and great-grandson of the founder.

As the years have gone by Victorinox and its competitor Wenger have had to spend increasing amounts of time – and money – in fending off the counterfeiters. The current case in the United States, which dates back to 1992, is just the latest in a long series of lawsuits which have involved Germany, France, the US, Spain and Japan.

Reading module – 2

In this module you are going to:
- ★ find some information in a text.
- ★ read another text to see what it is about.
- ★ work on some groups of words from the first text.

A I didn't know that

Work in groups of three.

Read the text **Marriage**. Find three things that you already knew.
And find three things that you didn't know.

The age of the single parent

MARRIAGE

IMPORTANT changes in women's attitudes to marriage and divorce are revealed by the report. Marriage is becoming less popular in the 1990s, and more wormen are choosing to marry later. "The institution or marriage is weakening in the European Community," it states.

"More and more women are living alone and bringing up children alone. These changes are having an impact on the economic activity of women, who often now must bear sole responsibility for their families," it concludes.

The marriage rate has fallen in every country of the EC. Between 1980 and 1992, the marriage rate in the Community dropped from 6.4 to 5.6 per thousend. French and Italian women have been the fastest to turn their backs on the institution of marriage and the Portuguese the slowest.

Since 1980 too, the number of marriages ending in divorce has increased. The divorce rate in the Community has gone up from 1.4 to 1.6 per thousand, with the United Kingdom and Denmark registering the highest rates and Spain and Italy the lowest.

Significantly, during the 1980s women have been taking the decision to marry later. The average age of woman at their first marriage rose in every EC country, from 23.2 years in 1980 to 25.1 in 1990.

Danish women are the most reticent about taking the decision, the average age for women there is 27 and a half, with UK and Greek brides anxious to tie the knot before they are 24.

Not only are increasing numbers of women turning their backs on the traditional role of a wife, but for many the decision to become a mother is being taken much later. Many women see single life as attractive, with 14.8 per cent of women EC-wide aged between 20 and 39 living alone.

There is a also a definite trend towards women having children later on in life. In 1990, the average age for a woman to have her first child was over 27 in the Netherlands and the UK (compared with 25+ in 1980), but under 25 in Greece and Portugal (23+ in 1980).

In most other EC states the average age is around 26.

More and more women also feel able to bring their children up alone. Some 6.5 per cent of all woman are single parents, compared with only 0.4 per cent of men. The highest incidence is in the UK where 10.1 per cent of women between 20 and 39 are single parents. Lowest are Ireland (2.3 per cent) and Greece (2.4).

Births outside marriage are also soaring. In 1980, only nine per cent of births were illegitimate, but in 1992 the figure was 20 per cent.

In Denmark, where there are many cohabiting couples, nearly half of all births are illegitimate and in France and the UK a third of all births are outside marriage. The lowest number of births outsides marriage occurs in Greece and Spain.

Three things from the article we all knew already before we read it.

1 ______________________
2 ______________________
3 ______________________

Three things we all learnt from the article.

1 ______________________
2 ______________________
3 ______________________

Now compare your answers with your partners.

B What is it about?

This text has the title **LONGEVITY**.

What does this mean? Is it a good title? Why? Why not?

SOCIETY THE EUROPEAN

The changing face of a European woman

Living longer, working harder

LONGEVITY

A FASCINATING insight into the changing role of women in the European Community in the last decade has been revealed in a report by the EC's statistical office, Eurostat, writes Sandra Smith.

Women make up 51.2 per cent of the EC's 350 million population, with little variation from country to country. In every country women outnumber men; by the highest proportion in Portugal and Germany, and the lowest in Ireland.

Women can also expect to live at least six years longer than men, thus as the population's age increases so does the ratio of women to men. In the 60-79 age group there are 132 women per 100 men; at 80 there are 223.

There is however, some good news for European men. Life expectancy for both sexes is rising steadily in all member states, and this is expected to continue.

In 1990, life expectancy at birth in the Community was 79.4 years for women (72.3 in 1960) and 72.8 years for men (67.4 in 1960).

The two main causes of death among women are diseases of the circulatory system (which cause nearly half all female deaths), and cancer (21.4 per cent). Breast and womb cancer cause more than one death in five, of women aged 35 to 54.

Social protection varies enormously from country to country, the survey found. In Denmark women receive 28 weeks of maternity leave; in Portugal 90 days.

During that time Danish women are paid a full salary. In Ireland it is as low as 70 per cent. The highest maternity benefits are paid in Luxembourg, Denmark and France; the lowest in Greece.

Marriage is declining in popularity and there has been a subsequent rise in illegitimate births – no fewer than 20 per cent in 1992.

An increasing number of women are also choosing to live on their own, and bring children up on their own.

Although women are catching up with men in gaining higher education, women form just 41 per cent of Europe's workforce, and many work part-time.

The widespread availability of childcare facilities (as in Denmark) also makes a major difference to whether women can go out to work, the report emphasises.

C Groups of words

Here are nine words or phrases from the text in **A**. Can you make three groups of three?

cohabiting • bringing up children alone • bride • single parent • marriage • living alone • to tie the knot • illegitimate • births outside marriage

1 ______ ______ ______

2 ______ ______ ______

3 ______ ______ ______

Reading module – 3

In this module you are going to:

★ decide in general terms what this article is about.
★ find information about a range of attitudes to the topic and their effect.

A What is the question?

Look at the cartoon. What is the question missing from the last picture?

B What is the title?

Work in a group of three.

Read through the article and make up a title for it.
Compare your title with the titles from the other groups.
Go back to the cartoon. Do you want to change your question?

Early sex education in the Netherlands has led to fewer pregnancies, writes Sandra Smith

Ask a nine-year-old British child how he came into the world and he may shyly tell the folk-story of a stork carrying a miraculous bundle in its beak. Speak to his Dutch equivalent and the chances are he will boldly explain what children in the Netherlands learn from the age of four – everything you wanted to know about sex.

But to the argument that such explicit sex education makes Dutch children dangerously wise beyond their years, there is a statistical rebuttal: the Netherlands has the lowest rate of teenage pregnancies in Europe.Well-informed, but apparently not promiscuous, Dutch teenagers begin sexual relationships on average six months later than the British, who top the European league in teenage pregnancies.

In a recent World Health Organisation report on 19 countries, the overwhelming conclusion reached was that sex education does not encourage promiscuity but can actually delay a youngster's first sexual experience.

"Those countries that rated most highly on openness about sex were also those that experienced the lowest birthrates," says the report.

Dr. Mariella Baldo, a WHO scientist, added: "Teaching young people about sex is like teaching someone to drive. You know that they at least will have a better chance of avoiding a crash."

In the Netherlands, a rise in teenage pregnancies in the 1970s spurred the authorities into action. Sex education is a compulsory part of the school curriculum from the age of 12, but most schools start much earlier. The unofficial philosophy seems to be "the sooner, the better".

Some parents fear that the Dutch system of explaining such issues to children as young as four is stripping them of their innocence. Others reason that innocence is dead anyway: that in a world where sexual images dominate the media, children must be able to come to terms with what they see on television and read in books.

Depending on such sources for primary information can lead to strange conclusions. A recent survey by the University of Rome revealed that 15 to 20 per cent of Italian teenagers learned about sex from television, newspapers and books. Fiver per cent thought that making love standing up was the best method of birth control.

Not all European governments are as eager as the Dutch to legislate on explicit sex education. After five decades of debate, Italian schools are still waiting for legislative guidance. The closest Italy came to a law was the Information and Sexual Education in Schools Bill, drafted in 1992, but parliament was dissolved before the senate could vote on it.

Under the proposal, schools were not actually required to include sex education on their syllabuses. Instead, teachers were encouraged to integrate the subject with more familiar topics such a history, art and biology.

In Italy and other European countries, the influence of the Roman Catholic Church is critical. Outgoing education minister Rosa Russo Jervolino, for example,believes that the state should not tamper with the traditional role of the family in sex education. In 1992 she supported the idea of school lessons in birth control, but reserved the rights of parents to say "no".

Parental rights and traditional values are also dominant in Britain. Parents have the right to withdraw their children from sex education classes, and the discussion of subjects such as HIV and other sexually transmitted infections has been removed from the national curriculum.

At present, sex education for the under-11s is not compulsory, and basic teaching

C Attitudes

Work in a group of three.

Fill in the box with information about one or two countries.

	Official attitude to this topic
Netherlands	
Italy	
Britain	
Germany	

Find out from your colleagues in other groups the information about the other countries. Check what they tell you.

Is there any evidence that these attitudes affect behaviour?

ɔr those at secondary school is left to ıe judgment of school governors.

ı Germany, responsibility for sex ducation lies with individual Länder with the result that there is a onsiderable disparity between the rotestant north and the Catholic ɔuth.

ı Würzburg, Bavaria, sex education lasses are compulsory in social cience classes, but only start when udents are 15. But in Protestant chleswig-Holstein., the issue is rmly established on every school urriculum. There, children learn bout sex from the age of eight in a pecial sex education courses.

rom teaching about parts of the ody, the syllabus moves on to sychology a year later at nine, xamining puberty and the different ates of development between boys nd girls.

he course gradually becomes more ophisticated, and by the school-aving age of 16 includes moral alues, unwanted pregnancies, Aids, nd protection against sexually ansmitted diseases. Written exams re taken from the age of 12.

Teenage Pregnancies
Latest Council of Europe figures for teenage pregnancies per 1,000 females aged 15-19

United Kingdom	32.9	Luxembourg	11.8
Portugal	22.7	France	9.3
Greece	19.9	Belgium	9.3
Ireland	16.1	Italy	8.9
Germany	12.4	Denmark	8.8
Spain	12.1	Netherlands	4.8

Writing module – 1

A letter from a friend

In this module you are going to:

- ★ identify some of the language of formal and informal letters.
- ★ correct some mistakes in a letter of invitation from one friend to another.
- ★ write a final version of this letter.

A Formal or informal?

Work alone, then in a group of three.

Which of these phrases might you find in an informal letter from a friend?

I am writing to inform you that . . .
I thought you might like to know that.
See you soon!
Yours faithfully
Yours sincerely
With best wishes
Thank you for your letter of 3rd July.
It was really good to hear from you.

Compare your answers with your partners.

B Check a letter

Here is a letter which some friends of yours have written to an English couple, Penny and John Richards, they met on holiday last year. They have asked you to help them with their English and have circled some things they found difficult. What changes would you make?

C The final version

Your teacher will now read out the final version of this letter. Write it down.

Dear Sir and Madam

We are thinking to write for a long time – in fact for more than half a year. As you can see it, we are not very good to keep in touch!
Since we come back from our holiday last year, many exciting things happen here. Eduard has now a new job as the manager of a computer shop, and the biggest news is that we expect a baby in November.
How is your health? We hope you are good.
We can still remember the wonderful time together on holiday and want to see you again. Why don't you coming to visit us here in summer? We have big flat with plenty of spaces for visitors.
We look forward to hearing from you.

Yours sincerely

Writing module – 2

Replying to an invitation

In this module you are going to:

★ identify some of the language of formal and informal letters.
★ correct some mistakes in a reply to an invitation from one friend to another.
★ write a final version of this letter.

A Formal or informal

Work alone, then in a group of three.

Which of these phrases might you find in an informal letter from a friend?

I am very grateful for your kind invitation.
Thank you very much for inviting me.
Dear Sir/Madam
Dear Friend
Unfortunately I have a previous engagement and so will be unable to attend.
I shall be delighted to take part.
I'd love to come.
I'm sorry but I won't be able to come because . . .

Compare your answers with your partners.

B Check a letter

Your friends have received a letter inviting them to spend a week at the home of an English couple they met on holiday last year. They have asked you to help them with their reply. What changes would you make to their letter?

Dear Friends

Thank you very much for your really kind invitation for spending a week with you. We would love to see you again and it would be wonderful visiting your part of England.
Unfortunately, there may be a problem. As you know it, Cristina expects a baby in November and we are not sure if she will be fit enough to travel all the way to England. Do you mind if we get in touch with you a bit nearer the time. We really hope it will be possible to come.

With very best wishes

C Follow up letter

A month later Cristina and Eduard have made up their minds. Write the letter they send to their English friends either to say *yes they can come*, or to say *no they can't*.

Compare your letter with your partners.

Writing module – 3

A formal complaint.

In this module you are going to:

★ identify some of the language of formal and informal letters.
★ check a letter of complaint to a hotel to see if there are any mistakes.
★ write a final version of this letter.

A Formal or informal?

Work alone, then in a group of three.

Which of these phrases might you find in a formal letter to a company?

Dear Manager
Dear Sir/Madam
Dear Mr Ryder
I have been meaning to write for ages.
I am writing in connection with . . .
I am writing to confirm the following booking which I made by telephone.
Have you heard from Sam recently?
I look forward to your early reply.
Looking forward to hearing from you soon.
Yours sincerely
Yours faithfully

Compare your answers with your partners.

B Check a letter

Antje Miedema has just been on a visit to the INTEX factory in Gloucester. The hotel she stayed at was not very good so she has drafted this letter to them. What changes would you make?

INTEX
The Manager
Red Lion Hotel
Watergate
Gloucester GL1 3PQ
England

Dear Sir/Madam

I stayed in your hotel on Tuesday and Wednesday night last week. Unfortunately I had a number of problems which I must draw to your attention.
Firstly when I arrived on Tuesday evening at 9.30 in the pouring rain there was no space left in your car park and I had to park almost 500m away and carry my luggage. I was then told that it was too late to get any food except for a sandwich.
On Wednesday morning the wake-up call I had booked did not come through so I was late for my appointment with the area manager of my company.
Finally on Thursday morning when I wanted to check out, you refused to accept a Eurocheque in payment of the bill although the amount was covered by my cheque card. I therefore had to walk – again in the pouring rain – to a bank, queue for 10 minutes, and then walk back with the cash. As a result I almost missed my ferry connection in Dover.
I feel that the standard of service you offer is completely unsatisfactory. You may be sure that I will not recommend your hotel to my colleagues visiting Gloucester in future.

Yours faithfully

C Write a letter

Write a letter like Antje's to the manager of the worst hotel in Europe – real or imaginary.

Interaction module – 1

In this module you are going to:

- ★ decide what Ana Vazquez would have done in different everyday situations in different countries.
- ★ give reasons for your choices.
- ★ describe an everyday situation in your country in which people from other countries might do the wrong thing.

A What did Ana do?

Work alone.

Read the following descriptions of three different everyday situations.
Ana knows that people behave differently in everyday situations in other countries.
She particularly wanted to do the right thing in each of these situations.
Decide what Ana did in each situation.

In the course of collecting data for the new INTEX brochure, Ana Vasquez went on business trips to all of the INTEX subsidiaries including the INTEX centre in Cairo. After she had come through the customs check at Cairo airport, she walked into the Arrivals Hall holding her briefcase in her left hand and her handbag in her right hand. She saw someone holding up a board with her name written on it. The person holding it was Youssuf Sharif, the Egyptian Personnel Officer from INTEX. He smiled when he saw Ana, walked up to her and held out his hand.

What did Ana do next?

1 Say *Hello, nice of you to come and meet me*, and show him that she had her hands full?
2 Put down her briefcase and shake hands with her left hand?
3 Kiss him on both cheeks?
4 Transfer her handbag to her left hand and shake hands with her right hand?

Last year Ana and Ralf decided to spend their summer holiday on a small Greek island. Neither Ana nor Ralf speak Greek so Ana bought a Greek phrase book at the airport. One day they visited a small taverna in the mountains. The waiter came to their table and started speaking to them in Greek. Ana wanted to gesture to him to wait a moment until she had found the right Greek phrase in her phrase book.

What did she do next? Read on; page 134.

1 Hold out her left hand with the palm facing towards the waiter.
2 Smile, shake her head and hold up the forefinger of her right hand.
3 Hold out both arms at her sides and look upwards.
4 Stretch out both hands with the palms facing towards the waiter.

When Ana went to England to visit Alison Steadman at the INTEX centre in Gloucester, Bruce Page, the Production Manager at the Gloucester Centre invited Ana for a drink at **The Fountain**, a popular pub near the cathedral. After they had parked their car in the pub car park, they walked towards the door of the pub.

What did Ana do?

1 Hold the door open and follow Bruce into the pub.
2 Wait for Bruce to open the door for her and go into the pub before him.
3 Wait for Bruce to open the door and go into the pub after him.
4 Open the door herself and go into the pub first.

B Giving reasons for your choice

Work in a group of three.

Discuss your choices with your partners. Give reasons why you chose one possibility and why you didn't choose the other possibilities. Here are some structures to help you.

I think Ana would have shaken Youssuf's right hand because that is the polite thing to do in Egypt.
I don't think Ana would have kissed Youssuf on both cheeks because people don't do that in Egypt.

If Ana had shaken Youssuf's left hand, he might have felt unhappy.
I'm sure that Youssuf would have been offended if Ana had shaken his left hand.

C Describing a situation in which people from other countries might do the wrong thing

Work with a partner.

Choose an everyday situation in your country or in another European country in which you think a person from another country might do the wrong thing.

Describe the situation simply like this:

You go into a shop . . . you ask the shop assistant . . . she says . . . .

Then describe four possible actions like this:

Would you
- a give her the money?
- b ask to speak to the manager?
- c kiss her hand?
- d shake her hand?

Work with a group of six people.

Read out the description of your situation to the other people in your group, then read out the possible actions.
Ask them to decide what they would do in this situation. Explain what you would do in this situation.

Interaction module – 2

In this module you are going to:
- ★ match complaints with responses in particular situations.
- ★ say what happened before and after a two-line dialogue.
- ★ role-play a situation where you are making a complaint or responding.

A Matching complaints with responses

Work on your own and with a partner.

Check the meaning of the following shopping vocabulary.

shrunk • heel • sell-by date • label • receipt • washing instructions

Compare your answers with your partner.
Now try and match the following complaints with the correct response on page 136.

COMPLAINTS

1 *We've been waiting twenty-five minutes and we haven't ordered yet.*

2 *I want to complain about this sweater. I've only washed it once and it has shrunk so much that I can't get it on.*

3 *I really must complain about the way you repaired these shoes. I have only worn them once and the heel has fallen off.*

4 *I bought this last Friday and when I got home I found that the last twenty pages were missing.*

5 *I bought this bacon here yesterday and when I got home I noticed that it was past its sell-by date. Can you change it for me?*

6 *I want to make a complaint about this bag of rice. When I opened it, I found more than a dozen little pieces of stone mixed in with the rice.*

RESPONSES

- ❑ *Oh, I'm awfully sorry, sir. Would you like to take another pack from the shelf?*
- ❑ *Could I just have a look at them, madam?*
- ❑ *Did you follow the washing instructions on the label, sir?*
- ❑ *I'm awfully sorry, madam. Would you like me to get you another bag or would you like to speak to the manager.*
- ❑ *I'm extremely sorry but we are very busy this evening, sir.*
- ❑ *I'm afraid we can't replace books unless you've got the receipt, madam.*

Check your answers with your partner.

B What happened before and after?

Work with a partner.

Decide with your partner for each of the six dialogues above.

- Who was talking?
- Where were they talking?
- What was said before the first line of the dialogue?
- What was said after the last line of the dialogue?

C Role-play

Work with a partner.

Role-play one of your completed dialogues to another pair in your group.

Interaction module – 3

In this module you are going to:
- ★ write the missing words in short dialogues.
- ★ write an A to Z list of your own experience of other cultures.
- ★ make generalisations about aspects of other cultures.
- ★ agree or disagree with your partner's generalisations about aspects of other cultures.

A Missing words

Work on your own and with a partner.

You are going to hear some short dialogues. Listen to the tape and write the missing words in the correct places.

- ● I think the French tend to drink more wine than beer.
- ▼ I ______________ say that; it depends ______________ the region of France you are talking about.
- ● The English have a ______________ to eat potatoes with every meal.
- ▼ I'm not ______________ that's true any longer. Things have changed a lot in the last ten years.
- ● In the majority of ______________ German beer is stronger than Irish beer.
- ▼ I'd go ______________ with you there.
- ● In my experience most Italians ______________ to eat their evening meal later than the Norwegians.
- ▼ Yes, ______________ agree with you there.
- ● I've heard that the Czechs tend ______________ to eat many vegetarian dishes.
- ▼ No, I ______________ they don't.
- ● Austrians tend to prefer coffee ______________ tea.
- ▼ Is that really the ______________ ? When I was there on holiday last winter, everyone seemed to be drinking tea.
- ● I read somewhere that the Japanese ______________ not ______________ use their hands when they are talking.
- ▼ That's ______________ true. When I was in Tokyo last year, they didn't appear to use any gestures at all.

Check your answers with your partner.

B Your own experience of other cultures

Work with a partner, then on your own.

The second person who speaks in each dialogue agrees or disagrees with the generalisation the first person makes.
Which statements are based on the speaker's own direct experience?
Which statements are based on what the speaker has read or heard?
Discuss your answers with your partner.

Write down the letters of the alphabet. You are going to make an A to Z list of your experience of other cultures.
For each letter of the alphabet write down the name of something or someone from another culture which begins with that letter.
Only write down the names of things or people from your own personal experience.

Here are some suggestions to help you.

a monument or a building you have visited • something you can drink • something you can eat • a car • something you can wear • tools • towns you have visited • people whose names you don't know • people whose names you know • a piece of equipment you use • restaurants, hotels or cafés you have visited

C Making generalisations about aspects of other cultures and agreeing or disagreeing with your partner's generalisations

Work with a partner.

Exchange A to Z lists with your partner.
Take it in turns to ask your partner about what he/she has written for each letter.
When your partner has explained what it means, try and make a generalisation about it.
Your partner will then agree or disagree with you based on his or her experience.

Here are two examples to help you:

1

You	*Why did you write "Swatch" for the letter S?*
Your partner	*Because I bought one when I was on holiday in Switzerland last year.*
You	*In general Swiss watches tend to be very reliable.*
Your partner	*I'd agree with you there.*

2

You	*Who is Mr Jones?*
Your partner	*He was the manager of the hotel we stayed at in England last year.*
You	*I think English people tend to be extremely reserved.*
Your partner	*I don't think that's true. I've met more talkative people in England than anywhere else.*

Listening module – 1

In this module you are going to:

- ★ make notes about the stories in a radio news broadcast.
- ★ re-write a news story.
- ★ write headlines for each of the news stories.

A Making notes

Work in a group of three.

You are going to hear a radio news broadcast. For each news story (1 – 4) you hear, one person is going to write down all the names in the story, another person is going to write down all of the places and the third person is going to write down all of the numbers. The news broadcast is in three parts: the main aspects of the four news stories; the full stories; a short summary of each story.

	Names	Places	Numbers
1	______	______	______
2	______	______	______
3	______	______	______
4	______	______	______

When you have listened to the news once, reconstruct each story with your partners using the notes you have made. Listen to the news again. Check your version of the stories with the other groups.

B Re-writing a news story

Work on your own.

Read the following statement that the bank robbers made to the police. Re-write each sentence as you heard it in the news broadcast.

We stole a white BMW half an hour before the robbery.
A white BMW was stolen half an hour before the robbery.

We parked the stolen car on the pavement outside the bank.
______

I threatened the cashier with a revolver.
______

I told the cashier to put the notes into a shopping bag.
______

I fired a shot in the air as a warning.

____

I drove the getaway car at 60 m.p.h. through the shopping precinct.

____

We knocked over two pedestrians during our escape.

____

The police caught us trying to bury the money in a cornfield.

____

C Writing headlines

Work with a partner

Imagine that the four news stories you have heard are written in a newspaper.
Write a typical newspaper headline for each story. Do not use more than ten words for each headline. Compare your headlines with the headlines other people in your group have written.

Listening module – 2

In this module you are going to:

- write down the missing information from a caller's message on a telephone answering machine.
- write down the callers' messages on telephone answering machines.
- write down the pre-recorded message and the caller's message on a telephone answering machine.

A Writing the missing information

Work on your own and check your answers with a partner. Listen to the first message and write the missing information on the form below.

Bristol Omnibus Lost Property

Article	______________
Description	*Leather, light brown, initials P.J.T. in gold letters*
Name	______________
Address	______________
Post Code	______________
Telephone Number	*01225/*

B Writing down the callers' messages

Work on your own and check your answers with a partner. Listen to the next two messages and complete the notes.

Caller's message 1

NAME OF CALLER ________________

CALLER'S TELEPHONE NUMBER ________________

MESSAGE

________ *appointment with Mr Grey* ________ *10.30 on* ________ .

Is it possible to ________ *appointment to* ________ *? If not* ________

please ________ *him.*

Caller's message 2

NAME OF CALLER ________________

CALLER'S TELEPHONE NUMBER ________________

MESSAGE

In Gloucester ________ *week on* ________ *. Staying at .* ________

in Northgate Street. What about drink or ________ *? Please leave* ________

at hotel.

C Writing down the pre-recorded message and the caller's message

Work on your own and check your answers with a partner. Write in the missing words in the **pre-recorded message**.

Pre-recorded message

Hello, this is the Broadwalk Dental Practice.

The ________ is closed now. If you have an

________ you can contact Mr Robertson on

Bristol ________ or alternatively

Ms Merryweather on Bristol ________ .

Please only call in cases of real ________ .

All ________ calls will be dealt with when

the practice is open again.

Please speak after the ________ .

Caller's name ________________

Message ________________

Listening module – 3

In this module you are going to:
- complete notes about an interview.
- explain the reasons for people's actions.
- discuss the meaning of phrases used in the interview.

A Completing notes

You are going to listen to an extract from a radio programme entitled "Working in Europe".
Guy Bradley and Silke Dantz-Bradley live in Bremen, in the north-west of Germany. Guy was born in Bath in the south-west of England. In this extract they are talking about their lives.

Work on your own and with a partner.

Guy talks about the different places where he has lived and worked. Listen to the interview and complete the following notes.

BATH	*Lived with parents/apprenticeship as stone mason and bricklayer/*
ADELAIDE	*Lived with . . . . /worked for . . . .*
BATH	*Lived with . . . . /couldn't find . . . .*
DELMENHORST	*Lived with . . . . in a . . . .*
	worked for . . . . building . . . .
BREMEN	*Lives in . . . . with . . . .*

B Explaining the reasons

Work on your own and with a partner.

Listen to the interview again and complete the following sentences:

1 *Guy lost his job with the local building firm in Bath because* ______________________________ .
2 *Guy decided to go to Australia because he wanted to* ______________________________ .
3 *Guy and his girlfriend went to Adelaide because* ______________________________ .
4 *Guy had to come back to England because he hadn't* ______________________________ .
5 *When Guy and his girlfriend went back to Britain they lived with his parents because* ______________________________ .
6 *When Guy lived in Delmenhorst, he went to the Volkshochschule because* ______________________________ .
7 *Guy doesn't want to go back to Britain to live because* ______________________________ .

C What does this mean?

Work with a partner.

Discuss the meaning of the following phrases from the interview.

Guy	*Jobs were like gold dust.*
Guy	*. . . to cut a long story short, we had to go back to Britain.*
Silke	*I am an only child.*
Guy	*We've got a much better standard of living here.*

Pronunciation module – 1

In this module you are going to:

- ★ identify foreign languages by their sound characteristics.
- ★ identify and practise rising and falling intonation in English speech.
- ★ identify and practise the stress pattern of English words similar to words in your language.

A Identifying foreign languages

Work on your own and with a partner.

You are going to hear six people introducing themselves in their own language. Try and match the speakers with the correct language.

Language	Speaker number
Italian	________
Japanese	________
Russian	________
Swedish	________
Turkish	________
Welsh	________

Check your answers with your partner.

Did you or your partner identify any languages which you can't speak? How did you identify them?

B Rising and falling intonation in English speech

Work on your own and with a partner. Listen to six different people saying *Good morning*. Does the speaker's voice go up or down? Tick the correct column.

	UP	DOWN
Speaker 1	______	______
Speaker 2	______	______
Speaker 3	______	______
Speaker 4	______	______
Speaker 5	______	______
Speaker 6	______	______

Check your answers with your partner.

Practise saying *Good morning* with a rising and a falling tune. You are going to hear two different speakers reading each of the following sentences once. Mark the words where the speaker's voice goes up like this ↗ and the words where the speaker's voice goes down like this ↘ .

1 Would you like tea or coffee?
2 Did he say *yes* or *no*?
3 We can have tomato soup or chicken soup.
4 They promised to come on Friday or Saturday.

Check your answers with your partner. Take it in turns to say the sentences aloud.
Now mark sentences 5 – 8 in the same way before you listen to the tape. Check your answers as you listen.

5 *Do you prefer red wine or white wine?*
6 *Shall we watch a film or go for a walk?*
7 *He can catch the six o' clock train or the eight o'clock train.*
8 *Would you prefer smoking or non-smoking?*

C The stress pattern of English words similar to words in your language

Work on your own and with a partner.

All languages use some words from other languages. On page 145 is a list of English words. Are any of them like words in your language? Write the similar words in your language next to the English words.

English	Your language	English stress pattern
academy		o-O-o-o
architecture		
atom		
altar		
democrat		
democracy		
dialogue		
dynamite		
electricity		
energy		
fatal		
initiative		
legal		
probable		
relative		

Sometimes the spelling is different and sometimes the pronunciation is different. Listen to the recording and draw the stress pattern for each of the English words e. g. Academy **o-O-o-o**

Check your answers with your partner. Say each of the words aloud and ask your partner to check your pronunciation.

Pronunciation module – 2

In this module you are going to:
- ★ identify and practise a rising-falling intonation pattern.
- ★ practise rising and falling intonation patterns with a list of items.
- ★ practise rising and falling intonation patterns with telephone numbers and spelling words aloud.

A A rising-falling intonation pattern

Work on your own and with a partner.

Listen to the speakers saying the following sentences.
In the first part of the sentence the speaker's voice rises like this:
I'll phone you ↗ . . . and falls in the second part of the sentence like this:
. . . when I get to the airport ↘ .

1 *If he doesn't come soon, we'll miss the train.*
2 *When the rain stops, we'll go for a walk.*
3 *I'm going to write to her after my exams.*
4 *Press the button, and wait for the door to open.*

Repeat the sentences. Try and imitate the speakers. Ask your partner to make a note of the differences between your pronunciation and the speakers' pronunciation.

B Rising and falling intonation patterns with a list of items

Work with a partner.

Listen to a customer and a barman talking in a pub. The customer's voice rises after each item she chooses from the menu and falls at the end of the sentence.

Barman	*Are you ready to order now, madam?*
Customer	*Yes. I'd like tomato soup ↗, roast chicken ↗, boiled potatoes ↗, cauliflower ↗, and chocolate gateau ↘.*

Repeat the dialogue with your partner. Choose different items from the menu below. Try and imitate the intonation of the two speakers.

The Crown, Marshfield – Lunch Menu

Starters

*Tomato soup * Chicken soup * Prawn cocktail * Egg mayonnaise*

Main Courses

*Roast beef * Rump steak * Vegetable curry * Roast chicken*

Vegetables

*Chips * Boiled potatoes * Peas * Carrots * Cauliflower*

Desserts

*Apple pie * Ice cream * Chocolate gateau*

C Rising and falling intonation patterns with telephone numbers and spelling words aloud

Work with a partner.

Listen to part of a telephone conversation between a hotel receptionist and a hotel guest.

Hotel receptionist	*Could you spell that for me, please?*
Hotel guest	*Yes, it's S ↗ – T ↗ – E ↗ – V ↗ – E ↗ – N ↗ – S ↗ – O ↗ – N ↘.*
Hotel receptionist	*And could you give me your phone number, Mrs Stevenson?*
Hotel guest	*Certainly. It's 0452 ↗ 525 ↗ 733 ↘.*

Repeat the conversation with your partner using your own name and telephone number.

Vocabulary module – 1

In this module you are going to:
- ★ match words for containers with pictures.
- ★ match words for containers with their usual contents.
- ★ match suitable adjectives with words for containers and their usual contents.
- ★ guess the name of a drink.

A Words for containers

Work on your own and with a partner.

Match the following words with the pictures.

glass • cup • bowl • pot • mug • jug • bottle • barrel • can • tin

Check your answers with your partner.

B Matching containers with their usual contents

Work on your own, and then with a partner.

Now match the following drinks with their usual containers e.g. pot + tea = a pot of tea

Some drinks can be matched with more than one container.

wine • water • tea • milk • juice • coffee • beer • soup • cider

Check your answers with your partner.

C Matching suitable adjectives with containers and their usual contents

Work on your own, then check your answers with your partner.

Now add one or two suitable adjectives to each combination of container + drink e.g.

(cup + tea) = a cup of tea + strong + lemon = a cup of strong lemon tea

Partner A	Partner B
spicy	milky
chilled	white
hot	de-caffeinated
strong	tomato
sweet	mineral
weak	lemon
cold	orange
fresh	red
dry	mushroom
sparkling	black

D Guessing the name of a drink

Work in groups of four.

Each person in the group chooses a favourite combination of a container, two adjectives and a drink. The other three people must try and guess the combination of words chosen by the fourth person. Each person can only ask five questions.

Here are some questions which may help you.
- *Would you drink this with a meal?*
- *Is this a winter drink?*
- *Could you drink this in a bar?*
- *Is it a non-alcoholic drink?*
- *What would you normally eat with this drink?*
- *Do you drink this on special occasions?*

Vocabulary module – 2

In this module you are going to:
- ★ talk about the comparisons people usually make in your language.
- ★ match the words used to make comparisons in everyday English.
- ★ match pairs of English words which are often used together.

A Comparisons

Work on your own and with a partner.

His hands were very cold.
His hands were as cold as ice.

The two sentences above say the same thing in different ways.
In the second sentence cold hands are compared with cold ice.

Write a list of three similar examples of comparisons in your own language. Discuss your list with your partner. The comparisons used in English will often be different from the comparisons used in your language.

B Comparisons used in everyday English

Work on your own and with a partner.

Check the meanings of any new words in the two lists below. Try and match the words in **List 1** with the correct words in **List 2**.

List 1	List 2
old	a judge
drunk	a sheet
strong	a mouse
cold	the hills
quiet	a lord
white	an ox
light	ice
sober	a feather

Now write the missing words in the following sentences:

1 This is the perfect rucksack for climbers; it's very strong but it's as light as a ______________ .
2 My great-grandfather used to sing that song – it's as ______________ as the hills.
3 I know he looks like a weak, old man but he is as ______________ as an ox.
4 His new friend is as ______________ as a mouse; she didn't say a word all evening.
5 After he had drunk the second bottle of wine he was as drunk as a ______________ .
6 When the doctor told him the bad news he went as ______________ as a sheet.
7 There was no heating in the waiting room and my feet are as ______________ as ice.
8 She went to the party but she stayed as ______________ as a judge because she only drank mineral water.

C Words which are often used together

"His hands were freezing cold." is another way of saying, "His hands were very cold."
Here are two lists of words which are often used together like freezing and cold.

Check the meanings of any new words in the two lists below.
Try and match the words in **List 1** with the correct words in **List 2**.

List 1	List 2
wide	new
dirt	wet
pitch	sharp
stone	cheap
soaking	asleep
rock	cold
blind	awake
razor	drunk
brand	black
fast	hard

Now write the missing words in the following sentences:

1 I made the coffee ten minutes ago; it's probably __________ cold by now.
2 It rained so hard that we were all soaking __________ in a few minutes.
3 I bought this coat in the market; it was __________ cheap but it's very warm.
4 It's pitch __________ in here; can you switch on the light?
5 This bread is rock __________ ; I can't get my teeth into it.
6 He's got a real alcohol problem; he gets blind __________ whenever he goes to the pub.
7 It's a brand __________ car; she only bought it yesterday.
8 I don't think the music will wake her; she's fast __________ .
9 Be careful you don't cut yourself with that knife; it's razor __________ .
10 I set my alarm clock for six-thirty so I was wide __________ at seven.

Record Chart Block Three Session 17 – 24

At the end of each session, record what you have done.

		From the Module Banks	
Session 17	Grammar ❑ __________	________ ❑ __________	________ ❑ __________
Session 18	Grammar ❑ __________	________ ❑ __________	________ ❑ __________
Session 19	Grammar ❑ __________	________ ❑ __________	________ ❑ __________
Session 20	Grammar ❑ __________	________ ❑ __________	________ ❑ __________
Session 21	Grammar ❑ __________	________ ❑ __________	________ ❑ __________
Session 22	Grammar ❑ __________	________ ❑ __________	________ ❑ __________
Session 23	Grammar ❑ __________	________ ❑ __________	________ ❑ __________
Session 24	Grammar ❑ __________	________ ❑ __________	________ ❑ __________

Evaluation Chart Block Three Session 17 – 24

Now that you have finished this block, think back over the work you have done in each area.

Which modules did you find easiest? Which hardest? Which areas do you need to concentrate on in your future work in English?

Fill in this chart to show how you feel about your performance in the seven areas covered by English for Europe. **This is your chart, for you.**

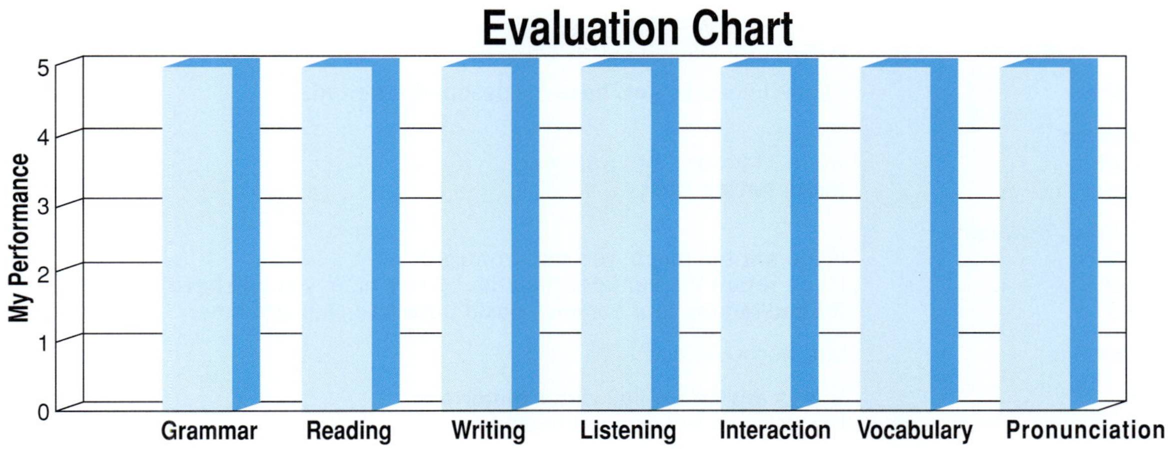

In each area, fill in the chart up to the number which you feel matches your performance.

Grammar

5 I knew all this already.
3 I knew some of this, but there was quite a lot of new material.
1 Nearly all the grammar we covered was new for me.

Reading & Listening

5 I understood everything.
3 I understood enough to answer the questions.
1 I didn't understand very much at all.

Writing

5 I can write what I want to say quite easily and without too many mistakes.
3 I know that my writing has some mistakes, but people can understand what I write.
1 I don't feel confident about writing in English. I find it hard.

Interaction

5 I can express what I want to say quite easily and without too many mistakes.
3 I know that when I speak English I make some mistakes, but people can understand what I say.
1 I don't feel confident about speaking English. I find it hard.

Vocabulary

5 I knew all this already.
3 I knew some of this, but there was quite a lot of new material.
1 Nearly all the vocabulary we covered was new for me.

Pronunciation

5 I think my accent in English is quite good.
3 I find some sounds in English quite difficult, but people can understand me.
1 I have a lot of problems with English pronunciation.

Grammar Terminology

	Examples
adjectives	good; expensive; dangerous
demonstrative adjectives	this; that; these; those
possessive adjectives	my; your; his; her; its; our; your; their
adverbs	extremely; individually; fast; hard
adverbs of frequency	once; twice; three times; sometimes
adverbials	in five years; at this time next year
articles	
definite articles	**the** book; **the** books
indefinite articles	**a** book; **an** English book
causatives	I think I need **to get/have** my passport renewed.
comparison	
regular	warm, warm**er**, (the) warm**est**
irregular	**good**, **better**, **best**
conditional/if-clauses	
type 1	If you **eat** too much, you **put** on weight.
type 2	If you **return** the car later than the agreed time, you **will have** to pay extra.
type 3	If I **had left** an hour earlier, I **could have had** plenty of time.
conjunctions	but; because; and
future	She is **driving** to Gloucester **tomorrow**. I'**m going to** relax on the beach. I'm sure that **will** help. It **won't be** too late to start.
future continuous	Bruce Page **will be catching** a flight from Birmingham.
genitives	Ana'**s** telephone number the number **of** the hotel
gerund/-ing form	She is wondering about hir**ing** a car.
infinitives	It's not too hard **to drive** on the left.
imperatives	Please **don't interview** staff from my department.
modal auxiliaries	can; could; shall; should; will; would ought to; have to; must/mustn't; needn't may; might
nouns	Alison; hotel; book; nationality
numbers	
cardinal numbers	one; two; three; four
ordinal numbers	first; second; third; fourth; fifth
objects	She calls **him**. I've got a message for **her**.
passives	The salt is added to the water. Our trip has been postponed.
past simple	When Ana **arrived** at her hotel in Gloucester, she **found** that Alison was not there.
past continuous	Ana arrived at her hotel in Gloucester while Alison **was taking** part in a meeting in another town.
past perfect simple	Ana arrived at her hotel in Gloucester after Alison **had left** for a meeting in another town.
past perfect continuous	Martina **had been working** for INTEX for two years when she got married.

Grammar Terminology

	Examples
past participles	
regular	dump**ed**; decreas**ed**
irregular	**been**; **done**; **thrown**; **written**
pronouns	
indefinite	nobody; no one; everybody; everyone; somebody; anybody; something; anything; everything; nothing
personal	I; you; he; she; it; we; you; they
possessive	It's probably one of **hers**. **Mine** are all here.
reflexive	my**self**; your**self**; them**selves**
plurals	three book**s**; two countr**ies**; some bus**es**
plural words	trousers; jeans; pyjamas; glasses
prepositions	on; for; in; with; on the corner of; at; after; about; according to
with adjectives	I was amazed at how cold the weather was.
with nouns	I was excited about the trip.
with verbs	I was worried about finding my way in a strange city.
present simple	Intex **provides** good working conditions.
present continuous	What **is** your town **doing** to protect the local environment?
present perfect simple	**Has** the information **arrived** yet?
present perfect continuous	She **has been wondering** about hiring a car.
present participle	**Starting off** without buying petrol can be dangerous.
quantifiers	
countable	**a few** days
uncountable	**a lot** of snow; **little** traffic
questions	Aren't you going camping?
How- questions	**How** far is it? **How** do you get to work?
Wh- questions	**Where** does she work? **When** do you work? **Why** is Ana in Gloucester? **Where** was Alison then?
indirect questions	They want to know what the company produces.
question tags	You're going to Portugal this year, **aren't you**?
relative clauses	She is the one **who/that designs the brochure every year**. It's a kind ot brochure **which/that attracts many potential customers**.
reported speech	She told me that she travels a lot.
singular	**one** book; **a** cassette; **an** orange
subject	**She** is not in the hotel. **These faxes** are urgent. **You** can call her.
superlative	cheap**est**; earli**est**; **most** expensive
verbs	
regular	listen, listened, listened
irregular	be, was/were, been read /iː/, read /e/, read /e/
phrasal verbs	**Let** the cat **out**. She **gave up** her job.
phrasal prepositional verbs	You don't really **get on with** horses.
prepositional verbs	I am **waiting for** my sister.

Grammar Survey

adjectives
international; different; present; fast; cheap; early; easy

an	**international**	company
	different	countries
in her	**present**	job

	regular comparative	*regular superlative*
fast	fast**er**	the fast**est**
cheap	cheap**er**	the cheap**est**
early	earl**ier**	the earl**iest**
easy	earl**ier**	the earl**iest**
difficult	**more** difficult	the **most** difficult
expensive	**more** expensive	the **most** expensive

	irregular comparative	*irregular superlative*
good	**better**	**best**
a lot of	**more**	**most**
many	**more**	**most**

adjectives/adverbs with the same form
fast; hard

demonstrative adjectives

close in time & place	*distant in time & place*
this year	that week
these shoes	those countries

possessive adjectives
What is **your** name? **My** name is Maria.
What colour are **your** flags? **Our** flags are red white and blue.

I	you	he	she	it	we	you	they
my	your	his	her	its	our	your	their

adverbs
enough; too; badly; very; really; well

adverbs of frequency
never; always; often; usually; sometimes

adverbs of manner
We must produce the brochure **quickly**.
She drives **carefully**.

articles

idefinite article

	boat		aeroplane
	colleague		employee
a	director	**an**	invitation
	fax		office
	glass		umbrella

conjunctions
and; or; but; because

The heat is turned down **and** the pasta is cooked gently.
Shall we watch a film **or** go for a walk?
She has never been to England **but** hopes to go there soon.
Antje did not like the flat where they lived before **because** it was not big enough.

genitive
Ana**'s** house; the name **of** the hotel;
the men**'s** families; the client**s'** questions;
at the dentist**'s** at the chemist**'s**;
a bottle **of** red wine; a cup **of** coffee

numbers
1 one; 2 two; 3 three; 4 f**ou**r; 5 fi**v**e; 6 six; 7 seven;
8 eight; 9 nine; 10 ten; 11 eleven; 12 twelve;
13 thirteen; 14 fourteen; 15 f**i**fteen; 16 sixteen;
17 seventeen; 18 eighteen; 19 nineteen; 20 twenty;
21 twenty-one; 30 thirty; 40 f**o**rty; 50 fifty; 60 sixty;
70 seventy; 80 eighty; 90 ninety; 100 one/a hundred;
101 a hundred and one.

ordinal numbers
1st first; 2nd second; 3rd third; 4th f**ou**rth; 5th fi**f**th;
6th sixth; 7th seventh; 8th eighth; 9th ninth;
10th tenth; 11th eleventh; 12th twelfth;
13th thirteenth; 14th f**ou**rteenth; 15th fi**f**teenth;
16th sixteenth; 17th seventeenth; 18th eighteenth;
19th nineteenth; 20th twentieth; 21st twenty-first

prepositions

time
I will pick you up from the hotel **at** 8.15.
I won't be back in Gloucester **before** 7.30.
He would be happy to work for them **until** he retires.
I have been living in Lyon **for** two years.
They have been here **since** 15th December.

Note Detailed grammar explanations and practice you will find in **English for Europe Learner's Book** and in **99 Steps to Grammar and Usage**.

place & direction
Ana arrived **in** Gloucester yesterday.
A dinner party **at** Ana's house.
They live **near** Hamburg.
A car travelling **between** England and France.

Note *It is often not possible to translate prepositions literally. Therefore, idioms and phrases which include prepositions should be learned as a complete expression.*

verbs
speak; see; go; buy; pay; write

be

long form	***short form***
I am	I'm
you are	you're
he is	he's
she is	she's
it is	it's
we are	we're
you are	you're
they are	they're

The short form is more common in spoken English. The long form im more formal and is mostly used only in written English and in short answers.

Yes, I am. Yes, she is.

be ***in the past***

I	was
you	were
he/she/it	was
we/you/they	were

modal auxiliaries

can	You **can** get emergency medical treatment by dialling 100.
	I **could** have got a job as a space engineer.
had better	I'**d better** start making some travel plans.
had better not	I'**d better not** use that firm again.
have to	We will **have to** change our arrangements.
must	You **must** open a bank account.
	That **must** have been very interesting.
mustn't	You **mustn't** arrive late at a social event.
need	You **needn't** get a visa if you are a citizen of the European Union.
ought to	I think you **ought** to plan visits to all of them.
should	Applicants **should** be prepared to travel overseas to conferences.

The meaning of the main verb can be changed by using a modal auxiliary verb thus expressing a variety of speech intentions.

Note *Modal auxiliary verbs are always followed by a main verb, except in the case of short answers.*
(Yes, he should. No, she shouldn't.)

phrasal verbs
She wrote a letter of application and **sent** it **off** with a copy of her CV.
More and more women also feel able to **bring up** their children alone.

Note *Always learn the verb and the relevant preposition* (off; up; *etc) together.*

prepositional verbs
Look around your own home of office.
Carpets, tiles and rugs are **made from** our fibres.

Note *Always learn the verb and the relevant preposition* (around; from; *etc) together.*

phrasal/prepositional verbs
Where can I **find out about** concerts, films, etc?
She was **looking forward to** joining the company.

Note *Always learn the verb and the relevant adverb and preposition* (out about; forward to; *etc) together.*

tenses
present simple

I	work
you	live
he	works
she	lives
it	looks
we	drink
you	drive
they	eat

The present simple describes regular actions, habits and generally accepted facts relating to the present.

INTEX **has** seven centres in six European countries.
Ana **lives** in Brussels.
Maria Cellini **drives** to work every day.
It can be used to express a future action.
My ferry **leaves** at six o'clock tomorrow morning.

Negative statements and questions in the present simple are formed with **do/does**.

present continuous

I	am	listen**ing**
you	are	work**ing**
he	is	read**ing**
she	is	danc**ing**
it	is	wait**ing**
we	are	walk**ing**
you	are	writ**ing**
they	are	com**ing**

The present continuous describes something that is happening at this moment in time.

Antje and her boyfriend **are looking** for a flat.
She is **updating** the information about the company's locations in Europe.
It may also be used to express a future action.
I **am leaving** the company next week.
She is **meeting** me at the airport.

present perfect

I	**have**	**worked**
you	**have**	**seen**
he	**has**	**sent**
she	**has**	**finished**
it	**has**	**stopped**
we	**have**	**closed**
you	**have**	**waited**
they	**have**	**asked**

The present perfect is used to describe:

a *a state which began in the past and still exists in the present*
Ana and Ralf **have lived** her for a long time.

b *an action which has been repeated in the past*
Antje **has been** to France three times.

c *an action completed in the period leading up to the present*
They **have finished** the brochure.

present perfect continuous

I	**have been**	wait**ing**
you	**have been**	work**ing**
he	**has been**	talk**ing**
she	**has been**	writ**ing**
it	**has been**	rain**ing**
we	**have been**	travell**ing**
you	**have been**	talk**ing**
they	**have been**	read**ing**

The present perfect continuous is used to describe a state or action which began in the past and is still continuing in the present. Particular emphasis is placed on the duration of the action.

Maria's daughter **has been learing** to drive since last Christmas.
I **have been living** in Lyon for two years.

present participles

He saw the ship **going** down.

A present participle may be used to shorten a sentence.

past simple

I	wait**ed**	we	ask**ed**
you	call**ed**	you	lik**ed**
he	look**ed**	they	work**ed**
she	help**ed**		
it	clos**ed**		

but

I	drove
she	swam
it	flew

The past simple is used to describe actions and events which have been completed in the past.
Last week the government **increased** the tax on petrol.

Negative statements and questions in the past simple are formed with **did**.
Antje **did** not **like** the flat where they **lived** before.
When **did** you **move** to the place where you live now?

past continuous

I	**was**	listen**ing**
you	**were**	talk**ing**
he	**was**	laugh**ing**
she	**was**	work**ing**
it	**was**	snow**ing**
we	**were**	sing**ing**
you	**were**	say**ing**
they	**were**	ask**ing**

The past continuous is mainly used to describe actions which take place during a period in the past.
While Ana **was driving** to Gloucester she had a flat tyre.

The past continuous is also used to describe actions and events which were already in progress at a certain point in the past of were already in progress when another action or event started.
What **were** you **doing** on November 9th, 1989 when the Berlin Wall came down?

past perfect

I	**had**	**written**
you	**had**	walk**ed**
he	**had**	ask**ed**
she	**had**	**said**
it	**had**	finish**ed**
we	**had**	listen**ed**
you	**had**	wait**ed**
they	**had**	telephon**ed**

The past perfect describes actions which happened before a time in the past or states which existed before a time in the past.
Paolo Rezzi **had worked** for another textile firm before he joined INTEX.
She **had been** a student for five years before she joined the company.

past participles
regular asked; closed; drowned; hoped; waited

irregular been; caught; held; known; paid

*The past participle is used in the formation of the present and past perfect tenses (*he asked*;* had been*) and the passive (*is made*;* was reported*).*

future
will-future

I	**will**	**see**
you	**will**	**visit**
it	**will**	**rain**

The will-future is used to describe actions and states in the future and to express opinions, suppositions and speculations about them.
Further snow or sleet **will** fall over eastern parts of Poland.
I expect it **will** be alright.

future continuous

I	**will be**	travell**ing**
she	**will be**	wait**ing**
they	**will be**	sleep**ing**

The future continuous is used to describe an action which is in progress during a period in the future.
Where **will** you **be living** in ten years' time?

going to-future

I	**am**	**going to**	start
you	**are**	**going to**	arrive
she	**is**	**going to**	leave

The going to-future is used to express firm plans or intentions.
We **are going to take** the children to the seaside next weekend.

reported speech
"I **think** it **is** a quiet little place."
She said she **thought** it **was** a quiet little place.
"I **have** never **seen** such a beautiful cathedral."
She said she **had** *never* **seen** *such a beautiful cathedral.*
When the introductory verb is in the past most of the tense forms change in indirect speech.

present → past; past → past perfect;
present perfect → past perfect;
past perfect → past perfect; will → would;
may → might; can → could; shall → should

sentence types
affirmative statements
INTEX is a multi-national company.
She is fond of fish. Ana works in an office.
She can speak Spanish.

negative statements
She doesn't like the weather in Belgium.
They don't like shellfish.
They can't speak Russian.

questions		***short answers***
Is this the Brussels train?	–	Yes, it is.
Are you sure?	–	No, I'm not.
Do you know the number?	–	Yes, I do.
Does the train stop in Paris?	–	No, it doesn't.
Did she say, "Yes"?	–	Yes, she did.
Are they going to Belgium?	–	No, they aren't.
Is it raining?	–	Yes, it is.
Have you ever been to Lyon?	–	No, I haven't.
Has the rain stopped?	–	Yes, it has.

date
11th June, 1995; 11 June, 1995; June 11th, 1995; June 11, 1995

time
am *from midnight to midday*
pm *from midday to midnight*

capital letters at the beginning of a word the first person singular	I
names	Maria Cellini; Gloucester
countries	Wales; Denmark
nationalities	Welsh; Danish
festivals	Easter; Christmas
months	May; December
days of the week	Saturday; Sunday
forms of address with names	Ms Steadman; Mr Page
at the beginning of letters	Dear Ralf; Dear Sir/Madam
at the end of letters	Yours sincerely Best wishes

8B Community citizens living in another Member State

Nationals of	Living in											
	B	DK	D	GR	E	F	IRL	I	L	NL	P	UK
	1988	1988	1988	1987	1982	1988	1988	1988	1988	1988	1988	1985-1987
B	–	283	17 854	1 233	9 730	50 200	–	3 674	–	22 942	910	–
DK	2 094	–	12 519	1 123	5 451	2 440	–	1 110	–	1 298	348	–
D	24 304	6 320	–	10 693	39 066	43 840	–	24 517	–	39 400	4 133	43 000
GR	19 075	461	274 793	–	606	7 860	–	11 774	–	3 953	51	13 000
E	50 187	875	126 402	906	–	321 440	–	6 841	–	17 578	7 105	30 000
F	92 322	1 853	71 773	6 268	23 599	–	–	17 118	13 200	7 496	2 803	28 000
IRL	1 318	930	8 360	529	684	1 880	–	1 037	–	3 103	199	532 000
I	250 209	2 006	508 656	6 418	13 025	333 740	–	–	–	15 890	1 060	75 000
L	4 948	16	4 542	43	–	3 180	–	223	–	381	26	–
NL	60 825	1 763	96 881	2 685	13 821	13 980	–	4 405	20 450	–	1 546	20 000
P	10 554	272	71 068	336	31 012	764 860	–	1 936	32 900	7 766	–	13 000
UK	21 000	10 096	83 010	16 093	65 318	34 180	–	17 209	–	37 094	7 115	–
EUR 12	536 836	24 875	1 275 858	46 327	193 312	1 577 600	66 400	89 844	–	156 901	25 296	766 000
EUR 12 and in third countries	858 650	136 177	4 489 105	155 187	334 935	3 680 100	83 500	407 023	–	591 847	94 453	1 785 000

Commission of European Communities – Directorate-General for Audiovisual, Information, Communication and Culture, Brussels

Acknowledgements

Computer Graphics – Thomas Emde, Dortmund p. 14, 19, 26, 34, 52, 78, 79, 85, 102, 125

Drawings Linden Artists, London p. 32, 72, 93

Photos – Grafik/Fotodesign L. L. Bergmann, Berlin p. 20, 25, 28, 29, 38, 59, 62, 63, 64, 73, 75, 105, 107, 133, 134

AA Photolibrary, Hants, UK p. 18

Bavaria, Düsseldorf p. 9/SSI; p. 11/FPG; p. 12/SSI; p. 15/Stock Imagery, TCL, Picture Crew; p. 16/SSI, p. 17/Viesti; p. 18/Viesti, p. 21/TCL; p. 24/TCL; p. 29/Images, Panoramic Images; p. 31/SSI; p. 36/Panoramic Images; p. 37/Manuel Neuhaus p. 39/George French; p. 40/David Ball; p. 42/Tibor Bognar; p. 47/Panoramic Images; p. 53/FPG; p. 81/Panoramic Images; p. 90/Creastock; p. 91/Japack; p. 92/Neuhaus; p. 94/Benelux Press; p. 99/FPG; p. 100/Custom Medical, Photo Shot; p. 110/111/Keute; p. 112/Japack; p. 120/TCL; p. 122/TCL; p. 123/TCL; p. 130/Füllenbach; p. 137/FPG; p. 138/Lauter; p. 143/TCL; p. 144/Japack; p. 145/Japack; p. 147/Widmann, PRW, Japack, Photo Shot; p. 148/Japack

The Bell Educational Trust, Cambridge, UK. p. 60

Dr. Karl Wolfgang Biehusen, Vorwerk Dipshorn p. 42; 43

British Tourist Authority, Frankfurt/M. p. 142

J. Allan Cash, Ltd., London p. 12; 13; 35; 37; 41; 45; 50; 59; 67; 71; 100; 107; 116; 131; 139; 140, 141; 147

Comstock, Berlin p. 106; p. 110; p. 135; p. 136

dpa-Fotoreport, Frankfurt/M. p. 22/Wöstmann; p. 39/Baum; p. 42/Coopes van Haas; p. 44/Ossinger; p. 61/Backhaus-Pohl; p. 62/Barone; p. 67; p. 68/epa Lehtikuva; p. 69/Pressensbild; p. 105/Barone; p. 110, 111/P. A. Interpress; p. 113/Barone

Bildarchiv Huber, Garmisch-Partenkirchen p. 30

IFA-Bilderteam, Düsseldorf p. 28/Förster; p. 99/Diaf; p. 110/International Stock, p. 111/Int. Stock, p. 117/Int. Stock, p. 118/Int. Stock, p. 119/Int. Stock, p. 121/Int. Stock; p. 123/Diaf; p. 126/Int. Stock; p. 149/TPL

The Image Bank, Berlin p. 9/D.W. Productions; p. 10/Color Day Photography; p. 12/Richard Pan; p. 16/Franklin Wagner; p. 17/Garry Gay; p. 18/Max Schneider, Hans Neleman; p. 23/Garry Cralle; p. 38/Joe Saffold; p. 44/Steve Allen; p. 45/Robert Holland; p. 46/Daniel Kirk; p. 58/David de Lossy; p. 65/Romilly Lockyer; p. 66/Chuck Kuhn; p. 74/Larry Gatz; p. 80/Christian Kaiser; p. 81/Image Makers; p. 82/Andy Caulfield; p. 83/Philippe Sion; p. 88/Bernard Roussel; p. 89/Will Crocker; p. 91/Andy Zito; p. 94/Paul Biddle; p. 95/Harald Sund; p. 96/Will Crocker, Dag Sundberg; p. 97/Laurie Rubin; p. 100/Cran van der Lende, Laurie Rubin; p. 105/Juan Silva; p. 106/C. Irion; p. 108/Laurie Rubin; p. 109/Will Crocker, G&V Chapman; p.110/Clint Eley; p. 112/Grant V. Faint, Tim Bieber, Ellen Schuster; p. 114/Garry Gay, Yellow Dog Prods; p. 127/P.-E. Berglund; p. 132/Charles Weckler; p. 139/Steve McAlister; p. 146/Hess; p. 147/Jaime Villaseca, Nino Mascardi; p. 148/M. Tcherevkoff

Keystone Pressedienst, Hamburg p. 83; p. 113

Helga Lade Fotoagentur, Berlin p. 23/H.R. Bramaz; p. 42/Trippmacher; p. 65/Arand, Ott, Kirchner; p. 77/Morell; p. 84/TPH; p. 100/Reichert, Assmann, BAV; p. 110/Bergmann; p. 113/BAV; p. 115/Thompson; p. 117/BAV; p. 123/Interfoto, NDS, Steckenreuter, Reichert

Pictor International Bildagentur GmbH, Hamburg p. 92

Premium Stock Photography, Düsseldorf p. 49/K. Ballard

Christel Schneider, Hamburg p. 12

Victorinox, Switzerland p. 123, 124

Zentrale Farbbild Agentur GmbH, Düsseldorf p. 7/Ron Lowery; p. 10/Hauck, Amand; p. 26/B. Simmons; p. 33/Savage; p. 55/Frkovic; p. 56/Barton; p. 57/M. Keller, Barton; p.65/Kaufman; p. 86/Weber; p. 87/Diebold; p. 90/Taufic; p. 98/Kalt; p. 103/Probe; p. 114/CPA; p. 118/Foster; p. 120/Mug Shots; p. 128/Skelley; p. 140/Nelson; p. 144/Masahiro Sano; p. 145/Seman Design Group

Texts – The European, 200 Gray's Inn Road, London p. 20/17.12.93; p. 34/14.1.94; p. 42-43/23.9.94; p. 69/14.11.94; p. 76/regular feature; p. 78-80/16.12.94; p. 84-85/4.2.94; p. 87-88/21.10.94, 18.11.94, 2.12.94, 16.12.94; p. 89/regular feature; p. 124-125/23.9.94; p. 126-127/3.12.94; S. 128-129/8.4.94 (cartoon after Min Cooper)